M000308813

**AA**

# walking in the Scottish Highlands

First published 2006

Produced by AA Publishing
© Automobile Association Developments Limited 2006

Published by AA Publishing (a trading name of Automobile Association Developments Limited, whose registered office is Fanum House, Basing View, Basingstoke, Hampshire RG21 4EA; registered number 1878835)

Ordnance Survey® This product includes mapping data licensed from Ordnance Survey® with the permission of the Controller of Her Majesty's Stationery Office.
© Crown copyright 2006. All rights reserved. Licence number 399221

ISBN-10: 0-7495-4850-9
ISBN-13: 978-0-7495-4850-6

A02781

A CIP catalogue record for this book is available from the British Library.

The contents of this book are believed correct at the time of printing. Nevertheless, the publishers cannot be held responsible for any errors or omissions or for changes in the details given in this book or for the consequences of any reliance on the information it provides. This does not affect your statutory rights. We have tried to ensure accuracy in this book, but things do change and we would be grateful if readers would advise us of any inaccuracies they may encounter.

We have taken all reasonable steps to ensure that these walks are safe and achievable by walkers with a realistic level of fitness. However, all outdoor activities involve a degree of risk and the publishers accept no responsibility for any injuries caused to readers whilst following these walks. For more advice on walking safely see page 112.

Some of these routes may appear in other AA walks books.

Visit the AA Publishing website at www.theAA.com/bookshop

Layouts by Liz Baldin at Bookwork Creative Associates Ltd, Hampshire, for AA Publishing

Printed by Leo Paper Group in China

PREVIOUS PAGE: *Highland scenery near Torridon Village*

# **walking** in the
# Scottish Highlands

Discover sheltered sandy beaches, glistening lochs and dramatic mountain scenery

AA

# Contents

*This superb selection of walks introduces the themes and characters that define the dramatic landscape of the Scottish Highlands.*

# Introducing the Scottish Highlands

The line between the smooth Lowlands and the sudden lifting of the mountains runs from the south end of Loch Lomond around to Inverness. Here, narrow roads twist through mountain passes and beside the lochs, and towering summits rear overhead. The Great Glen, the dramatic fault which slices Scotland in two, is part of a landscape which never fails to impress. A land of extremes, it holds Britain's deepest area of fresh water, the highest mountains and the most Arctic environment – on the Cairngorm plateau around Ben Macdhui.

## Northeastern Highlands

From Rannoch Moor, a vast expanse of treacherous peat bog, to Glencoe village, the majestic mountain pass of Glen Coe, with the rocky summits of the Three Sisters, is one of the most spectacular sights in Scotland. In summer, a trip on the ski-lift to the 2,400-ft (731-m) summit of Three Sisters will be rewarded by spectacular views over Rannoch Moor and the surrounding mountains.

Beyond Glencoe, the roads along the banks of Loch Leven provide some of the area's finest views. To the north, Ben Nevis, Britain's highest mountain, at 4,406ft (1,343m), dominates the scene. The route to its summit is challenging but on a clear day, the views are spectacular – the line of the Great Glen, the distant Cuillins on Skye and, very occasionally, the coast of Ireland. Further north lie the Cairngorms, where outdoor enthusiasts can find skiing, canoeing, mountaineering, cycling and walking. Alternatively, the dramatic mountain scenery can be viewed from aboard the Strathspey Steam Railway.

In the Great Glen you'll find sea, lochs and mountains all converging on a congenial city, set beside the Moray Firth. Inverness, the 'Capital of the Highlands', sits on the northeastern extremity of the Great Glen and the banks of the River Ness. Southwest from Inverness lie the dark waters of Loch Ness; to the east, the desolation of Culloden; to the west, the mudflats of Beauly Firth.

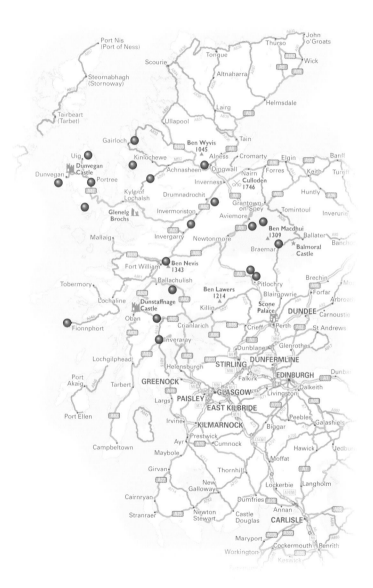

The Great Glen is a spectacular geological fault, running from the Firth of Lorne to the Moray Firth, cutting Scotland in two. Loch Ness forms a major part of the Caledonian Canal, which follows the line of the Great Glen. The loch contains more water than all the lakes and reservoirs in England and Wales put together. It is 24 miles (38km) wide and 750ft (228m) deep. The medieval Urquhart Castle, once captured by Edward I and then held by Robert the Bruce, guards the Great Glen, perched atop a rocky promontory.

## The Western Highlands and Islands

From space, Scotland north of the Forth and Clyde looks like a loosely woven cloth – an ancient tartan perhaps. Here, high mountains and deep glens, tumbling seas and shimmering lochs, open moorland and spreading forests lure you. This vast area is sparsely populated but it teems with wildlife from red deer, wild cats and otters to an astonishing variety of bird life. Scattered ruined cottages remain, from when the landlords drove the locals from the land in favour of sheep.

The coastline of Scotland from Mull to Loch Broom breaks down into a succession of sea-grit promontories and sea lochs. Inland, there is a hinterland of mountains, moorland, miles of wilderness, waterfalls, lochs and glens.

The 'road to the Isles' ends at the busy fishing harbour of Mallaig, which is also the terminus of the West Highland Line, one of Britain's most scenic railways. Knoydart, across Loch Nevis, accessible only by sea, provides wild and wonderful walking country.

From the picture-postcard village of Plockton, look north to the rugged hills of the Applecross peninsula. The breathtakingly spectacular road to Applecross reaches some 2,050ft (625m). Further north, around Gairloch, the road winds around the bay and eventually turns into a track, leading to the former lighthouse at Rubha Reidh. To the south are intriguing woody inlets, perfect for exploring by boat.

Inland, the scenery is equally spectacular – southwest of Inverness, the broad Strath Glass leads to the village of Cannich, where four valleys meet. Eastwards, down Glen Urquhart, is the prehistoric Corrimony Cairn, with its standing stones. Glen Cannich is entered by

## using this book

### Information Panels
An information panel for each walk shows its relative difficulty, the distance and total amount of ascent (that is how much ascent you will accumulate throughout the walk). An indication of the gradients you will encounter is shown by the rating ▲▲▲ (fairly flat ground with no steep slopes) to ▲▲▲ (undulating terrain with several very steep slopes).

### Minimum Time
The minimum time suggested is for approximate guidance only. It assumes reasonably fit walkers and doesn't allow for stops.

### Suggested Maps
Each walk has a suggested map. This will usually be a 1:25,000 scale Ordnance Survey Explorer map.

### Start Points
The start of each walk is given as a six-figure grid reference, prefixed by two letters indicating which 100km square of the National Grid it refers to. You'll find more information on grid references on most Ordnance Survey maps.

### Dogs
We have tried to give dog owners useful advice about how dog friendly each walk is. Please respect other countryside users. Keep your dog under control at all times, especially around livestock, and obey local bylaws and other dog control notices. Remember, it is against the law to let your dog foul in many public areas, especially in villages and towns.

### Car Parking
Many of the car parks suggested are public, but occasionally you may find you have to park on the roadside or in a lay-by. Please be considerate when you leave your car, ensuring that access roads or gates are not blocked and that other vehicles can pass safely. Remember that pub car parks are private and should not be used unless you have the owner's permission.

### Maps
Each walk is accompanied by a sketch map drawn from the Ordnance Survey map and appended with the author's local observations. The scale of these maps varies from walk to walk. Some routes have a suggested option in the same area with a brief outline of the possible route. You will need a current Ordnance Survey map to make the most of these suggestions.

a winding road between bare mountain tops, with groves of birch and alder. South along Loch Beinn a 'Mheadhoin' are parking places with many fine walks from them. Beyond the loch you can walk onto Loch Affric – a magical scene of hills and pine forest. In autumn, there is dazzling colour and the hint of snow on them. Follow the track through the mountains to Shiel Bridge and you're nearly at the coast again.

## Walking in the Highlands

In this book, you'll find a couple of summits – but mostly these are coastal routes, forest trails and walks that go around or through passes, instead of up. Even so, take care, as the paths are harder here. Some of the peaty trods, unchanged since the days of cattle drovers, will be more tiring and the longer and higher routes need to be treated with respect.

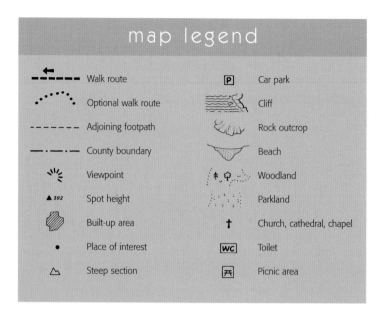

| map legend | | | |
|---|---|---|---|
| ← - - - - - | Walk route | P | Car park |
| •••••• | Optional walk route | | Cliff |
| - - - - - - | Adjoining footpath | | Rock outcrop |
| - · - · - · - | County boundary | | Beach |
| ☼ | Viewpoint | | Woodland |
| ▲ 392 | Spot height | | Parkland |
| | Built-up area | † | Church, cathedral, chapel |
| • | Place of interest | WC | Toilet |
| △ | Steep section | 🚻 | Picnic area |

*BELOW: Inveraray and Loch Fyne*
*RIGHT: Moonen Bay, Isle of Skye*

*Looking along Loch Awe from Cruachan Reservoir, Britain's biggest energy storage system.*

# The Hill with the Hole

The scenic Cruachan Reservoir collects rainfall from a fairly small catchment, just 9 square miles (23sq km), bounded by the rocky ridge of Ben Cruachan. This rugged walk takes you through lovely woodland to the impressive Falls of Cruachan, with superb views of Loch Awe along the way.

*ABOVE: Kilchurn Castle, Loch Awe*
*RIGHT: View of Ben Cruachan from Monument Hill*

## The Big Battery

But Cruachan is more than just a rather small power station. It's a rechargeable storage system for electrical energy, a very big electric battery. The demand for electric power varies from day to day, and even from minute to minute; the surge at the advertising break during your favourite soap, as a million kettles get switched on at once.

Coal and oil power stations can be stoked up or cooled off, but only quite gradually. Nuclear stations run at the same rate day and night and the greenest energy sources, wind and wave generators, give power according to the weather. So, there has to be a way of taking electricity out of the National Grid when there's too much, and putting it back when it's most needed.

*BELOW: Kilchurn Castle, Loch Awe*
*RIGHT: Ben Cruachan*

## Cruachan Power

Fortunately, an electric generator running backwards becomes a motor, and a turbine turns into a pump. At 'white-meter' (off-peak) times of day, water is pumped from Loch Awe up to Cruachan Reservoir, 1,000ft (305m) above. At 7:15pm on weekday evenings, it flows back again.

The stored energy in the battery of your car is sufficient to keep it running for about half a minute, but that's enough to start it in the morning and run the tape deck when the engine's off. Full to the brim, Cruachan Reservoir, with the capacity of about half a billion car batteries, in theory holds enough potential energy to supply the UK's peak demand for 10 minutes. In fact, the water can't be drawn down that fast, but at full flow Cruachan can supply 400 megawatts, enough for most of Glasgow. Time your arrival for 7:15pm, and you could see the reservoir sinking at an inch (2.5cm) per minute. The same amount of water will be flowing out into Loch Awe, just beside the visitor centre. The whole process – pumping up and then retrieving the potential energy – is not much more than 50 per cent efficient. The waste heat ends up in Loch Awe, where it benefits the fish farm that is located opposite the visitor centre.

## The Secret Source

The Cruachan powerhouse makes a fairly small impact on the outer world. Around 12 miles (19km) of pipes bring water into the reservoir, and the outgoing or incoming electricity loops across the hill on high pylons. The 1,030ft (315m) dam is only visible once you reach the corrie; the power station itself is actually buried deep in the heart of the mountain. So you can still enjoy the gorgeous scenery undisturbed by the furious activity going on beneath your feet.

## walk information

| | |
|---|---|
| ➤ **DISTANCE** | 2 miles (3.2km) |
| ➤ **MINIMUM TIME** | 1hr 45min |
| ➤ **ASCENT/GRADIENT** | 1,200ft (365m) ▲ ▲▲ |
| ➤ **LEVEL OF DIFFICULTY** | 林 林 林 |
| ➤ **PATHS** | Steep, rugged paths, 2 ladder stiles |
| ➤ **LANDSCAPE** | Wooded slopes and high corrie |
| ➤ **SUGGESTED MAP** | OS Explorer 377 Loch Etive & Glen Orchy |
| ➤ **START/FINISH** | Grid reference: NN 078268 |
| ➤ **DOG FRIENDLINESS** | Good, but high and steep ladder stiles to negotiate |
| ➤ **PARKING** | Two pull-ins on north side of A85, opposite visitor centre. Also lay-by ½ mile (800m) west. Not visitor centre car park |
| ➤ **PUBLIC TOILETS** | Cruachan Visitor Centre |
| ➤ **CONTRIBUTOR** | Ronald Turnbull |

## walk directions

1 Two paths run up on either side of the **Falls of Cruachan**. Both are initially rough and steep through woodland. The western one starts at a tarred lane opposite the entrance to the power station proper (not the visitor centre, slightly further to the west). This diminishes to a track, which becomes rough and crosses the railway as a level crossing. A path continues uphill in steep zig-zags through birch, rowan and oak. There are various points to stop and take a look along **Loch Awe**, which disappears glittering into the distance. White speckled stones in the path bed are Cruachan granite. The path continues steeply to the top of the wood.

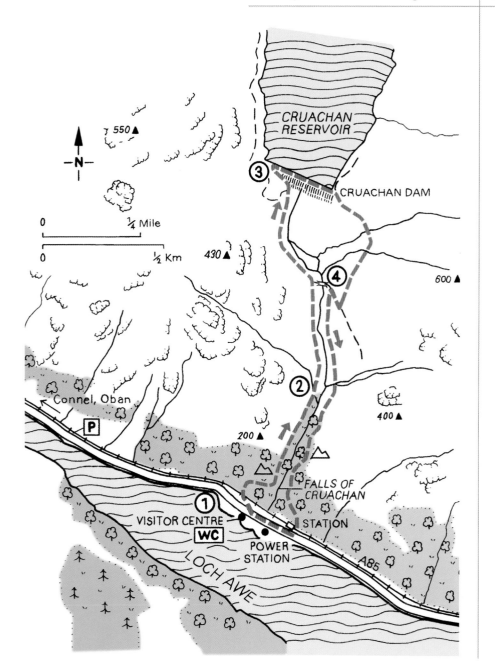

2 Here, a high ladder stile crosses a deer fence. With the stream on your right, continue uphill on the small path to a track below the **Cruachan dam**. Turn left, up to the base of the dam, which measures 1,030ft (315m) wide and 150ft (46m) high. Because it's tucked back into the corrie, it can't be seen from below, but it is clearly visible from the top of Dun na Cuaiche, 12 miles (19.3km) away. The hollows between the 13 huge buttresses send back a fine echo. Steps on the left lead up below the base of the dam, then iron steps take you on to the dam's top.

3 From here you look across the reservoir and up to a skyline that's slightly jagged at the back left corner, where Ben Cruachan's ridge sharpens to a rocky edge. In the other direction, your tough ascent is rewarded by a long view across the low country of Lorn. Turn right to the dam end, where a track leads down right for some distance to reach a junction, then go right for 50yds (46m).

4 At this point you could stay on the track to cross the stream just ahead, leading to the top of the path used for coming up. You might wish to do this if you are concerned about the ladder stile on the main route. There is no clear path as you go down to the left of the stream, to reach this high, steep and slightly wobbly ladder stile. Below this there is a clear path that descends grassy slopes and gives a good view of some of the **Falls of Cruachan**. Inside the wood, the path becomes steep and rough for the rest of the way down. Just above the railway, it turns to the left, then passes under the line by a low tunnel beside **Falls of Cruachan Station**, to reach the **A85** below.

RIGHT: *Looking out from Barguillean Farm towards Ben Cruachan*

*A tough but rewarding walk
past the Half-way Lochan
and the great north corrie
of Nevis.*

# Half Ben Nevis

*ABOVE: Across Loch Linnhe lies Fort
William, sheltered by Ben Nevis*

For 21 years in the 19th century, an observatory was sited on the summit of Ben Nevis. It recorded, to the surprise of few, that this is one of the wettest spots in Britain. Averaged over the year, the summit is sunny for about two hours each day.

This walk of half the hill shows you the mountain's great northern crags and the rocky hollow of Coire Leis. The further edge of the corrie is the jagged line of Tower Ridge, Britain's longest rock climb. In early spring, the damp Atlantic winds coat the crags in thick hoar-frost, over which climbers with crampons and ice axes have created hundreds of routes.

## Chamber of Clouds

Charles Wilson, a grammar school teacher turned Cambridge professor, came to Ben Nevis on holiday in 1894. The Scottish-born professor was so struck by the effects of sunlight on the clouds above Coire Leis that he attempted to reproduce them in the Cavendish Laboratory. In so doing, he invented the Wilson cloud chamber, for which he was awarded the Nobel Prize for Physics in 1927.

In summer, the moist Atlantic air that sweeps into Coire Leis condenses into cloud, and then rain. Each droplet forms around a 'nucleation centre' such as a speck of dust. Perfectly clean air can become supersaturated: it has more than enough moisture to form clouds, but can't. When moist air rises up Ben Nevis it expands due to the drop in pressure. As it expands it cools, allowing the water droplets to appear. In Wilson's Cloud Chamber, the pressure drop was achieved by means of a bicycle pump working backwards. One pull of the pump handle, and any passing particle became suddenly visible as a pencil-line of white cloud. The step-up in size is astonishing: it's as if a small model aeroplane left a vapour trail as wide as the solar system and visible to an observer on another star!

Cosmic rays – high energy particles from outer space – can be seen zipping through the cloud chamber. Thus the positron (the positive electron) was discovered in 1932 and the muon (an exotic heavy electron) in 1937. It is actually possible to make your own Wilson cloud chamber – simply cool air with dry ice and shine a torch in. The successor to the cloud chamber was devised while gazing into a glass of beer. Donald Glaser earned the Nobel Prize for his bubble chamber in 1960.

*RIGHT: Ben Nevis, viewed from the Caledonian Canal at Corpach*

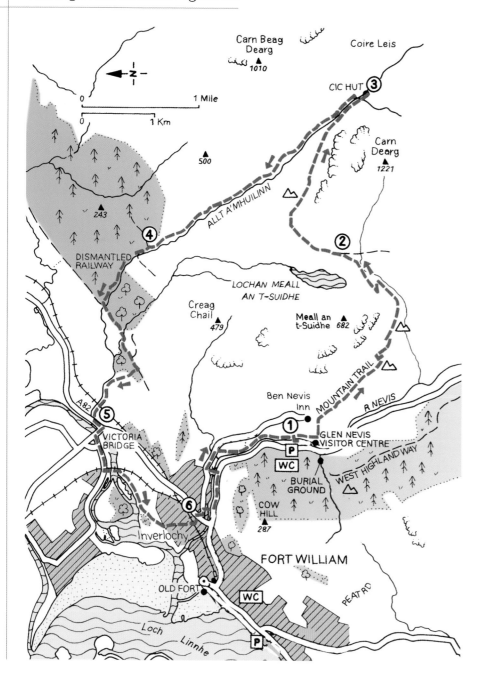

## walk directions

1 At the downstream corner of the car park, a bridge signed 'Ben Path' crosses the **River Nevis**. The path turns upstream, crossing fields to join the **Mountain Trail** (formerly known as the Pony Track) to Ben Nevis. After a long climb, a notice points you to a zig-zag up left on to the half-way plateau. The path passes above **Lochan Meall an t-Suidhe**, the Halfway Lochan, down on the left.

2 The main path takes a sharp turn back to the right, heading for the summit. Your smaller path descends ahead, behind a wall-like cairn. Soon it climbs gently over peat bog to a cairn on the skyline. Here it becomes rough and rocky, as it slants down across the steep slide slope of the valley of **Allt a' Mhuilinn**. Eventually it joins the stream and runs up beside it to the **Charles Inglis Clark (CIC) Hut**.

## walk information

| | |
|---|---|
| ➤ **DISTANCE** | 10 miles (16.1km) |
| ➤ **MINIMUM TIME** | 6hrs 15min |
| ➤ **ASCENT/GRADIENT** | 2,000ft (610m) ▲ ▲ ▲ |
| ➤ **LEVEL OF DIFFICULTY** | 🚶 🚶 🚶 |
| ➤ **PATHS** | Hill paths, well-built, then very rough, 6 stiles |
| ➤ **LANDSCAPE** | Slopes of Britain's biggest hill |
| ➤ **SUGGESTED MAP** | OS Explorer 392 Ben Nevis & Fort William |
| ➤ **START/FINISH** | Grid reference: NN 123731 |
| ➤ **DOG FRIENDLINESS** | On leads through Achintee grazings, by River Nevis |
| ➤ **PARKING** | Large car park at Glen Nevis Visitor Centre |
| ➤ **PUBLIC TOILETS** | At start |
| ➤ **CONTRIBUTOR** | Ronald Turnbull |

**3** Return for 100yds (91m) and then cross the stream on the right to join a clear path which leads downhill. This descends a rocky step with a waterslide and reaches a ladder stile into plantations.

**4** Go down a forest road and where it bends left over a bridge, keep ahead down a rough path. This stays beside the stream to a ladder stile at the railbed of the old aluminium railway. Turn left for ½ mile (800m), when a side-track joins from the left and the track passes under power lines. In another 220yds (201m) take a smaller track on the right that rejoins the **Allt a' Mhuilinn** stream. Keep to the right of distillery buildings to reach the **A82**.

**5** Cross the **River Lochy** on **Victoria Bridge** opposite and turn left into a fenced-off side road and left again along a street. It rises to meet a railway bridge. Turn left here on to a long footbridge back across the **Lochy**. At its end, turn right over a stile to walk along a riverside path. This passes to the right of a rugby ground and then becomes a built path that leads into woodland. After two footbridges, bear left on a smaller path to the edge of **Inverlochy**. Turn right, then left into a street with copper beeches. This leads through **Montrose Square** to the **A82**.

**6** The street opposite is signed 'Ben Nevis Footpath'. Shortly, take a stone bridge to the Glen Nevis road. Turn left for ¼ mile (400m) to a track on the left. Recross the Nevis on a green footbridge and turn right to a lay-by marked 'No Overnight Parking'. Just beyond this, a small riverside footpath leads up-river to the footbridge at Glen Nevis Visitor Centre.

*LEFT: View of Ben Nevis from Bonarie*

*This superb walk uphill at the back of Braemar gives a taste of the Cairngorms.*

# Moorland on Morrone

ABOVE: *Robert Louis Stevenson's home in Braemar*
LEFT: *The Cairngorms rise beyond Loch an Mor and Rothiemurchus Forest*

Coming down the back of Morrone hill, you descend through several different plant zones, and the home ground of two distinctive Grampian birds, Ptarmigan and Grouse. The tundra shrubs that grow on the plateau belong to the heather family, but with oval leaves rather than needles. They can be easily distinguished during August, as their berries are conveniently colour-coded. The crowberry fruit is black, the cowberry red and the bilberry, also known as the whortleberry or blaeberry, has a juicy purple fruit and pale green leaves.

## Ptarmigan Territory

On the windswept, often snow-covered summit plateau, gravel alternates with shrubby plants that grow barely ankle-high. These are food for the ptarmigan, a bird of the grouse family that's rather like a small hen. Uniquely among British birds, it turns white in the winter, and in spring and early summer it will still be white in patches. Its late summer plumage is paler than the grouse, and more speckled, but the easy way to recognise it is by where it lives – a grouse above the heather line is a ptarmigan – and by its behaviour. It relies on camouflage and when you notice it, it will probably be standing on the gravel only a few yards away. Even then, it doesn't fly away, but will probably wander off round the back of a boulder. In springtime, the male bird's soaring display flight is accompanied by a soundtrack of belches and cackles. The 'P' at the beginning of its name is purely ornamental – in Gaelic it's tarmachan.

## Heather and Grouse

At 2,000ft (610m), bilberry grow, along with dwarf heather. Once you turn down on to slightly more sheltered ground, the heather springs up twice as high. At around 1,500ft (457m), it is deep enough to hinder off-path walking. Here, yellow tormentil and white woodruff are established, and you may see meadow pipits and mountain hare.

A small brown bird – or more likely three or four – leaps up out of the heather with a squawking cry that seems to say 'go back, go back!' Grouse go with heather, like pandas go with bamboo and koalas with gum trees. Red grouse are found only in the British Isles, and unfortunately their heather country, however familiar and tiresome to Scottish walkers, is rare and vanishing in a world context. The grouse

*RIGHT: Rothiemurchus Forest, with the Cairngorms in the distance*

need old, leggy heather to nest in, but shorter, younger plants to eat. As a result, grouse moors are burnt in a ten-year cycle to provide tall heather habitats, with short, fresh heather near by. The piebald effect of 'muirburn', as it's called, gives these lumpy hills an attractive extra texture.

Eighty per cent of the grouse's diet is heather, the rest being the insects that live in it. As birds lack teeth they require small stones in their gizzards to help grind their food up and aid digestion. For grouse, sharp quartz grit is ideal, and you may spot small piles of this beside the track.

## walk directions

1 Take the wide track uphill, to the right of the duck pond at the top of **Chapel Brae**, bearing left twice to reach **Woodhill house**. The house can be bypassed by taking a small footpath on the right, which rejoins the track just above. When the track forks again, bear left to reach a viewpoint indicator.

2 Cross a track diagonally to a hill path marked 'Morrone'. The path has been rebuilt with rough stone steps. Higher up, it slants to the right along a line of rocky outcrops, a geological dyke of harder rock. At the top of this it turns directly uphill, passing five sprawling cairns. These are the turning point in the Morrone Hill Race that is part of the Braemar Games. The wide, stony path runs up to the **radio mast** and other ugly constructions on the summit.

3 The summit, if you turn your back on the buildings, has fine views across Deeside to the high Cairngorms. On the main tops, Ben Macdhui and Beinn a' Bhuird, snow may show right through the summer. To the east you will see Loch Callater and the White Mounth plateau. A notable hump is Cac Carn Beag, one of the summits of Lochnagar. Morrone's summit area is bare stones, but if you go past the buildings you'll find the start of a wide track. It runs down to a shallow col and climbs to the cairn on the low summit

beyond. Here it bends left towards a lower col, but before reaching it, turns left again down the side of the hill. A gentle zig-zagging descent leads to the road by the **Clunie Water**.

4 Turn left, alongside the river, for 1½ miles (2.4km). Ben Avon, with its row of summit tors, fills the skyline ahead. After a snow gate and golf clubhouse comes a road sign warning of a cattle grid (the grid itself is round the next bend). Here a track, back up to the left, has a blue-topped waymarker pole.

5 Go up between caravans to a ladder stile with dog flap. A faint path leads up under birches, bearing right and becoming clearer. After a gate in a fence the path becomes quite clear, leading to a Scottish Natural Heritage signboard and blue waymarker at the top of the birchwood. The path becomes a track with a fence on its right and, in 220yds (201m), reaches the viewpoint indicator, Point ②. From here you return to the duck pond.

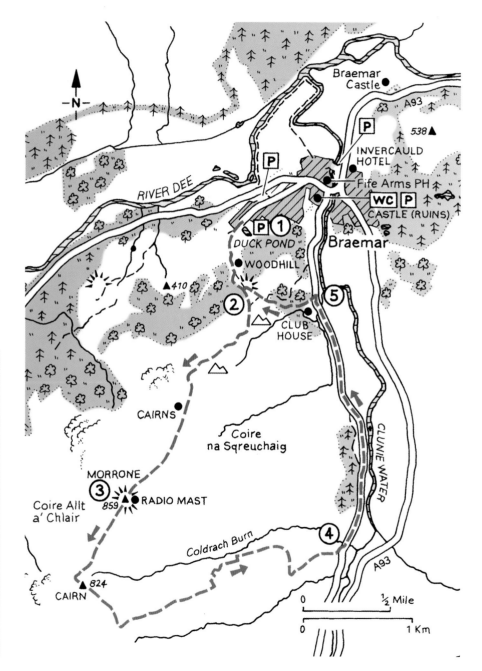

## walk information

| | |
|---|---|
| ► **DISTANCE** | 6¾ miles (10.9km) |
| ► **MINIMUM TIME** | 4hrs 15min |
| ► **ASCENT/GRADIENT** | 2,000ft (610m) ▲ ▲ ▲ |
| ► **LEVEL OF DIFFICULTY** | 🚶 🚶 🚶 |
| ► **PATHS** | Well-made but fairly steep path, track, quiet road section, 1 stile |
| ► **LANDSCAPE** | Rolling heather hills |
| ► **SUGGESTED MAP** | OS Explorer 387 Glen Shee & Braemar |
| ► **START/FINISH** | Grid reference: NO 143911 |
| ► **DOG FRIENDLINESS** | On leads in reserve, also on hill during grouse nesting May/June |
| ► **PARKING** | Duck Pond, at top of Chapel Brae, Braemar |
| ► **PUBLIC TOILETS** | Braemar centre (opposite Fife Arms) |
| ► **CONTRIBUTOR** | Ronald Turnbull |

*Along the shore of Loch Ness, past the home*
*of the Loch Ness Monster as well as a*
*different monster, the Beast of Boleskine.*

# Farigaig Forest and Loch Ness

ABOVE: *On the shores of Loch Ness*

It would be difficult for anyone but the most hardened sceptic to gaze out over the beautiful waters of Loch Ness without a small hope of seeing something, which might be interpreted as a 'sighting'. The first encounter with the Loch Ness monster dates back to the 6th century AD, when St Columba was crossing the River Ness. One of his companions was attacked by a water beast. When the saint ordered it to go away, it did. The onlookers, pagan barbarians whose friend had already been eaten, promptly converted to Christianity.

The account was set down 100 years later by Adomnan, an abbot of Iona. It sounds suspiciously like an earlier incident from the life of a different holy man, St Martin of Tours, and also like a story about how Christianity took over a site where human sacrifice had been offered to a river god.

Later confirmation came during the Lisbon earthquake of 1755. A shock wave, freakishly magnified along Loch Ness, sent breakers crashing against the shore at Fort Augustus – clearly Columba's monster was still down there disturbing the water.

## The Beast of Boleskine

Authentic sightings of a rather different monster did, however, take place along this walk in the early 1900s. Finding it fashionable to be Scottish, Alexander Crowley changed his name to Alesteir and bought the nearby hall to become the Laird of Boleskine. In his time, Crowley was known as 'The Beast of Boleskine', the 'wickedest man alive'. He identified himself with the Great Beast described in the final book of the Bible; the seven-headed monster that was to battle with the angels at the end of time.

In pursuit of his precept 'do what thou wilt shall be the whole of the law', he debauched minor film stars, betrayed his friends and became an alcoholic and heroin addict. At Boleskine, as he studied his magical grimoires, the sky darkened at midday so that candles had to be lit, and the lodge keeper went mad. We might take the darkening of the sky as a normal Scottish summer rain cloud, but we can still see the rowan trees that his neighbours planted to protect themselves from his magical influence.

Apart from seducing his neighbours and brightening the Inverness-shire scene with various exotic mistresses, Crowley contributed to local life by prankishly reporting to the Society for the Suppression of Vice the prevalence of prostitution in Foyers (where there wasn't any). He also made an impassioned plea against the plan to enclose the Falls of Foyers in hydro-electric water pipes.

*RIGHT: Urquhart Castle on the shores of Loch Ness*

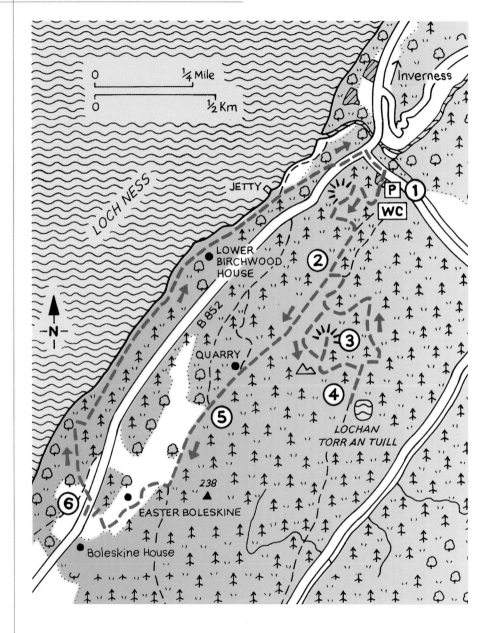

**1** From the car park, follow yellow waymarkers uphill near a stream. After 100yds (91m), a path on the right is signed 'Loch View'. After a bench, the path contours briefly then turns up left, to a higher viewpoint. It then turns back sharply left and descends on earth steps through a little crag to a forest road. Turn right for 200yds (183m).

**2** Turn up left on a footpath with more yellow waymarkers. The path has a low, heavily mossed wall alongside as it bends up to a higher forest road. Turn right and walk for about 150yds (137m) until you reach a sharp left-hand bend. Keep ahead here, on a small footpath through an area of cleared forestry, then go steeply up to the left under trees. At the top, bear left along a little ridge, dropping gently downhill to a viewpoint.

**3** Return for 100yds (91m) and bear left down the other side of the ridge. The path descends steeply to a forest road. A sign indicates **Lochan Torr an Tuill**, near by on the right, with a picnic table.

**4** Return down the forest road, past where you joined it. It climbs gently, then descends to the sharp right bend where you turned off earlier – the waymarker says 'to Car Park' on the side now facing you. After 150yds (137m), at another 'to Car Park' waymarker, turn left down the path with the low mossed wall to the forest road below (Point ②). Turn left, past a red/green waymarker. The track kinks left past a quarry.

**5** Where the main track bends right, downhill, keep ahead on a green track with a red/green waymarker. It emerges from the trees at a signpost. Follow this down to the right towards **Easter Boleskine house**. Green waymarkers indicate a diversion to the left of the house, to join its driveway track below. Follow this down to the **B852**.

| ➤ DISTANCE | 4¼ miles (6.8km) |
|---|---|
| ➤ MINIMUM TIME | 2hrs 15min |
| ➤ ASCENT/GRADIENT | 700ft (213m) ▲▲▲ |
| ➤ LEVEL OF DIFFICULTY | 🚶🚶 🚶🚶 🚶🚶 |
| ➤ PATHS | Waymarked paths and tracks, 2 steep sections, no stiles |
| ➤ LANDSCAPE | Hillside of mixed woodland |
| ➤ SUGGESTED MAP | OS Explorer 416 Inverness, Loch Ness & Culloden |
| ➤ START/FINISH | Grid reference: NH 522237 |
| ➤ DOG FRIENDLINESS | On leads for short stretch past Easter Boleskine |
| ➤ PARKING | Forest Enterprise car park |
| ➤ PUBLIC TOILETS | At start |
| ➤ CONTRIBUTOR | Ronald Turnbull |

6  Turn right for 50yds (46m). Below the left edge of the road is a tarred track. Turn down past a blue/green waymarker to cross this track, with two blue waymarkers leading into a path beyond. This passes down to the right of electricity transformers. At the foot of the slope, the main path bears right with a blue waymarker. It runs above the loch shore and joins a gravel track just below **Lower Birchwood House**. At a tarmac turning circle, an overgrown jetty on the left is great for monster-watchers. The tarred lane ahead leads up to the **B852**, with the car park just above on the right.

*RIGHT: Urquhart Castle, Loch Ness*

*Following Queen Victoria and Prince Albert into the great through route of the Grampians.*

# Blair Castle and Glen Tilt

Since humans first arrived, Tilt has been a natural highway. King Robert the Bruce marched down Glen Tilt in 1306 on his way to a minor defeat near Tyndrum. Some 200 years later, James V and Mary, Queen of Scots attended a deer drive in 1529, but the next monarch to complete the whole route was Queen Victoria. She came this way with Prince Albert on the third of their 'great expeditions' from Balmoral.

ABOVE: *A milestone in Killiecrankie on the way to Blair Atholl and Blair Castle*
RIGHT: *Blair Castle, Perthshire*

## Hill Walking

Along with the Christmas tree and the 'Scottish Baronial' style of architecture, multi-day hill walks were ideas introduced from Thuringia in Germany by the Prince Consort. Today we'd call it backpacking, but historically the packs were carried by ponies and so were the people for much of the way. Even so, 69 miles (111km) from Dalwhinnie to Balmoral in a day was a considerable trek. Two bagpipers forded the Tarff side-stream waist deep, playing all the time, while the Queen came behind on her pony, led by her special ghillie, John Brown.

## An Angry Duke

Kings and cattle thieves, soldiers and shepherds have used Glen Tilt for thousands of years, and its right-of-way status is self-evident. But in 1840, the then Duke of Atholl, whose castle lay at its foot, felt he could make his own law. He did, after all, boast Britain's only private army. He tried to turn back a botanical expedition lead by a certain Professor Balfour. The professor won the right to walk the route, and his victory is commemorated in a ballad:

> *'There's ne'er a kilted chiel*
> *Shall drive us back this day, man.*
> *It's justice and it's public richt*
> *We'll pass Glen Tilt afore the nicht,*
> *For Dukes shall we care ae bawbee?*
> *The road's as free to you and me*
> *As to his Grace himself, man'*

## Responsible Access

During the deer-stalking season (mid-August–October) reasonable requests from the estate will be respected by walkers. Such a request is made at Gilbert's Bridge.

RIGHT: *Falls of Bruar, Blair Antholl*

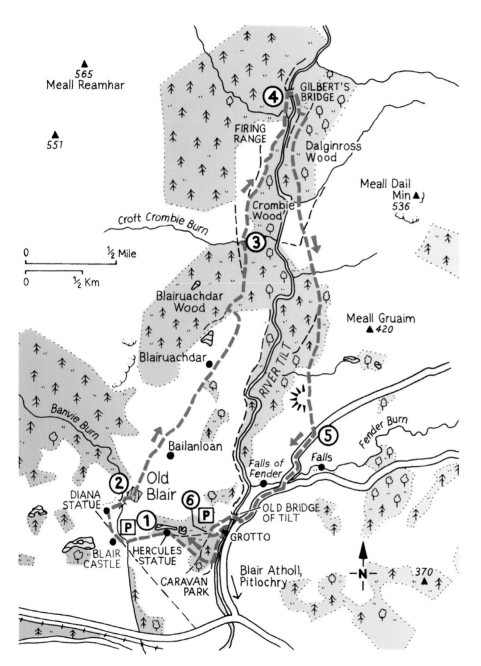

## walk information

| | |
|---|---|
| ➤ **DISTANCE** | 6½ miles (10.4km) |
| ➤ **MINIMUM TIME** | 3hrs 15min |
| ➤ **ASCENT/GRADIENT** | 852ft (250m) ▲▲▲ |
| ➤ **LEVEL OF DIFFICULTY** | 🚶 🚶 🚶 |
| ➤ **PATHS** | Estate tracks and smooth paths, 1 stile |
| ➤ **LANDSCAPE** | Castle grounds, woodland, wild river valley and mountains |
| ➤ **SUGGESTED MAPS** | OS Explorers 386 Pitlochry & Loch Tummel; 394 Atholl |
| ➤ **START/FINISH** | Grid reference: NN 866662 (on Explorer 386) |
| ➤ **DOG FRIENDLINESS** | On leads on open grazing land |
| ➤ **PARKING** | Castle main car park |
| ➤ **PUBLIC TOILETS** | Opposite driveway to castle |
| ➤ **NOTE** | Track through firing range closed on a few days each year (mostly weekdays). Consult Atholl Estate Ranger service |
| ➤ **CONTRIBUTOR** | Ronald Turnbull |

## walk directions

1 Turn right in front of the castle to a four-way signpost, and bear right for a gate into **Diana's Grove**. Bear left on a wide path to Diana herself. Turn right on a path that leads to a giant redwood tree, then bear left, to cross **Banvie Burn** on a footbridge alongside a road bridge. Go through a gate that leads to the road.

2 You are now at **Old Blair**. Turn right and follow **Minigaig Street** uphill. It eventually becomes a track and enters forest. Ignore a track on the left and, in another ¼ mile (400m), fork right. In 60yds (55m) you pass a path down to the right with a green waymarker. This is the return route if the firing range ahead is closed. Otherwise keep ahead to emerge from the trees at the firing range gate.

3 A red flag flies here if the range is in use, but read the notice carefully as on most firing days the track route through the range may be used. Follow the main track as it leads gently downhill, well below the firing range targets, until you get to the riverside, then fork right to reach **Gilbert's Bridge**.

4 Cross and turn right over a cattle grid. Follow the track for 220yds (201m), then turn left up a steep little path under trees to a stile. A green track now runs down-valley with fine views. It passes along the top of a mixed birchwood. Once through a gate into the wood, keep on the main track, gently uphill. After the gate out of the wood, there's a view across Blair Castle to Schiehallion. Another gate leads on to a gravel track and then a tarred road.

5 Turn right, down a long hill, crossing some waterfalls on the way down. At the foot of the hill turn right, signed 'Old Blair', to cross the **Old Bridge of Tilt**, then turn left into a car park.

6 Just to the right of a signboard, yellow waymarkers indicate a path that passes under trees to the **River Tilt**. Turn right through an exotic grotto until wooden steps on the right lead up to the corner of a caravan park. Head directly away from the river under pines. Ignore a track on the right and, at the corner of the caravan park, keep ahead under larch trees following a faint path. Cross a track to take the clear path ahead towards **Blair Castle**. Bear left at a statue of Hercules, passing the **Hercules Garden** (which you may walk round) to the front of the castle.

LEFT: *Central tower section of Blair Castle*

*A coastal walk to a raised beach called the Bile, then returning by way of Ben Chracaig.*

# Seeing Sea Eagles at Portree Bay

ABOVE: *Golden Eagle*

Portree is the capital of Skye, its colour-washed houses round the harbour pleasing on the eye. While walking beside the picturesque bay in Skye, keep at least one eye looking out to sea. You may spot what has been described as Britain's greatest ever wildlife conservation story.

## Sea Eagle Story

The last sea eagle in Scotland died on Skye in the early 1900s. Like all large raptors, it was shot at by shepherds and gamekeepers. An attempt to reintroduce them in 1959 was unsuccessful. In 1975, a secret RAF mission flew four young birds from Norway to the island of Rum. Over the next ten years, they were joined by 80 more. Today, about a dozen pairs are nesting, with a total population of around 100 spread up the western coast and the Hebrides.

In Gaelic it is called 'iolaire suil na greine' – the eagle with the sunlit eye – as its eye is a golden colour. In English it's also called the white-tailed eagle, the white-tailed fish eagle and the European sea eagle; it hasn't been back here long enough to finalise its name. Its nickname is the 'flying barn door' because it's so big, but it's not a heavy bird. Even with its 8ft (2.4m) wingspan, it weighs in at just 7lb (3kg). The sea eagle nests in cliffs. One nest, with an RSPB hide, is at Loch Frisa on Mull, another is here at Portree. The Aros visitor centre has a closed-circuit TV camera trained on the nest, and the Portree fisherman have taken to throwing seafood to the birds outside the bay. The eagle feeds by snatching fish out of the sea – but even more spectacular is its mating display, when the two birds soar and cartwheel high above the water.

## Was That An Eagle?

The first few eagles you think you see are almost certainly buzzards. When you see a real eagle, and even though you can't tell how far away it is, you'll know it for what it is. It's four times the size of a buzzard and its wingbeats are very slow and powerful. That's when it isn't gliding from one horizon to the other apparently without moving a feather. The sea eagle is even bigger than the golden one, and has a white tail – but so does a young golden eagle. However, if the eagle is flying over the sea, and especially if it's over the sea at Portree, then it's a sea eagle.

Naturalists believed that the bird's main problem would be the golden eagle, which during the years of extinction has taken over the nest sites. Sadly, the real enemy is still humans. In 2000, and despite a 24-hour guard, thieves took the two eggs from the Mull pair.

*LEFT: Portree Harbour, Skye*

## walk directions

1 Turn off the main **A855**, on a lane signed 'Budh Mor', down to the shoreline and continue to a small parking area. A tarred path continues along the shore. After a footbridge, it passes under hazels which show the ground-branching habit of bushes formerly coppiced, cut back every seven years for firewood. The path then rounds the headland to reach the edge of a level green field called **the Bile**.

2 A wall runs up the edge of the Bile. Ignore a small gate, but turn left with the wall on your right. Just before the field corner you pass a large fuchsia bush, spectacular in mid-summer. About 25yds (23m) later the path forks. Turn right, crossing a small stream and the wall, to head along the top edge of the Bile. Turn right, down a fence, to a field gate. Cross the top of the next field on an old green path, to a stile at its corner. You will see a track just beyond.

3 Turn sharp left, up the track. At the top, it passes through two gates to reach a stony road just to right of **Torvaig**. Turn left past the house and cross the foot of a tarred road into a gently descending track. It runs down between two large corrugated sheds and through to a gate with a stile.

## walk information

| | |
|---|---|
| ➤ **DISTANCE** | 2¾ miles (4.4km) |
| ➤ **MINIMUM TIME** | 1hr 15min |
| ➤ **ASCENT/GRADIENT** | 400ft (122m) ▲ ▲ ▲ |
| ➤ **LEVEL OF DIFFICULTY** | 🚶 🚶 🚶 |
| ➤ **PATHS** | Smooth, well-made paths, farm track, 3 stiles |
| ➤ **LANDSCAPE** | Views across Minch from wooded coast and hill above |
| ➤ **SUGGESTED MAP** | OS Explorer 409 Raasay, Rona & Scalpay or 410 Skye – Portree & Bracadale |
| ➤ **START/FINISH** | Grid reference: NG 485436 |
| ➤ **DOG FRIENDLINESS** | On leads through farmland, scoop poop on shore path |
| ➤ **PARKING** | Daytime-only parking on main A855 above Portree Harbour. Small parking area at slipway |
| ➤ **PUBLIC TOILETS** | Town centre |
| ➤ **CONTRIBUTOR** | Ronald Turnbull |

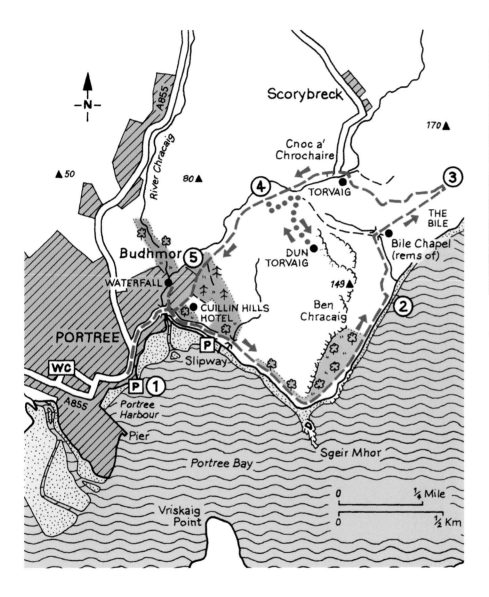

**4** The grassy path ahead leads down into Portree, but you can take a short, rather rough, diversion to **Dun Torvaig** (an ancient fortified hilltop) above. For the dun, turn left along the fence, and left again on a well-made path above. It leads to a kissing gate above the two sheds. Turn sharp right along the fence for a few steps, then bear left around the base of a small outcrop and head straight up on a tiny path to the dun. Remnants of dry-stone walling can be seen around the summit. Return to the gravel path, passing above Point ④ to join the wall on the right. The path leads down under goat willows into a wood where it splits; stay close to the wall.

**5** At the first houses (**The Parks Bungalow 5**), keep downhill on a tarred street. On the left is the entrance to the **Cuillin Hills Hotel**. A few steps later, fork right on to a stony path. At the shore road, turn right across a stream and at once right again on a path that runs up for 60yds (55m) to a craggy little waterfall. Return to the shore road and turn right to the walk start.

LEFT: *Boats at anchor in an inlet, Portree*
ABOVE: *Loch Portree with the houses of Portree scattered on the far shores*

*Dun na Cuaiche offers a fine view of Inveraray, the Campbell capital of Argyll.*

# Climbing to the Castle of Cups

Inveraray, on the shores of Loch Fyne, is the seat of the Duke of Argyll, chieftain of Clan Campbell. It is a fine example of town planning, created by the 3rd Duke of Argyll in the 1740s. The little town is stylish, with a wide main street of white-painted houses running up to the classical kirk (church). Thus it became, in the eyes of Campbells anyway, the capital of the southern Highlands.

*ABOVE: Dusk on Loch Fyne*
*RIGHT: The elegant castle and town of Inveraray on the shores of Loch Fyne*

# The Campbells Have Come

Until about 1600, the main power in the Highlands was MacDonald, Lord of the Isles. The 2nd Duke of Argyll aimed to take his place – by the normal methods of intrigue, betrayal and armed attack on neighbouring clans, but also by collaboration with the legal government in Edinburgh and the King in London. Clan Campbell would hit you with fire and the sword, but also with a writ from the Privy Council. As a result, they became the most powerful and the most universally disliked of all the clans.

In 1691, King William demanded an oath of loyalty from the rebellious Highland chieftains. MacIan of the Glen Coe MacDonalds was required to sign his oath in Inveraray. He hesitated over this visit to the capital of his hated rivals, and eventually arrived two days after the deadline. His delay was made the pretext for the Campbell-led Massacre of Glen Coe. When a Campbell was murdered in Appin 60 years later, the suspect, James Stewart of the Glens, was tried at Inveraray before a jury of Campbells, with Argyll himself as judge. The hanging of Stewart, who was almost certainly innocent, is still resented in the MacDonald country.

ABOVE: *Inveraray and Loch Fyne*
RIGHT: *Inveraray Castle was built in 1743 for the 3rd Duke of Argyll*

## Argyll Rebuilds

With the breaking of the clan system in 1745, the 3rd Duke of Argyll felt confident enough to pull down his fortified castle and rebuild in a style that suited a wealthy landowner who no longer needed to resort to violence to control his lands.

The present building, greatly admired by Sir Walter Scott, is described as a country house in the style of a castle. Its grey stone, quarried from just above the town, is sombre, but tones well with the muted green and blue of the Campbell tartan. To go with his new castle, Argyll decided he needed a new town. Some say that old Inveraray was simply too close to the castle. In its present position, curved around its bay, Inverary is a magnificent and early example of a modern, planned town. It is dominated by the Court House, where James of the Glens stood his trial, and by the white arches of the Argyll Hotel. One of these arches supplies a surprising passageway for today's A819 road.

The Duke of Argyll completed his ambitious rebuilding scheme with avenues and bridges; one of the bridges forms an elegant entry to the town on the A83. This walk crosses the Garden Bridge, designed by John Adam (1721–92) of the famous Scottish family of architects. The whole layout of castle and town is splendidly seen from the summit of Dun na Cuaiche (Castle of Cups).

| walk information | |
|---|---|
| ➤ DISTANCE | 4 miles (6.4km) |
| ➤ MINIMUM TIME | 2hrs 15min |
| ➤ ASCENT/GRADIENT | 900ft (274m) ▲▲▲ |
| ➤ LEVEL OF DIFFICULTY | 🚶🚶🚶 |
| ➤ PATHS | Clear, mostly waymarked paths, no stiles |
| ➤ LANDSCAPE | Steep, wooded hill, some rocky outcrops |
| ➤ SUGGESTED MAP | OS Explorer 363 Cowal East |
| ➤ START/FINISH | Grid reference: NN 096085 |
| ➤ DOG FRIENDLINESS | Must be under control |
| ➤ PARKING | Pay-and-display, Inveraray Pier |
| ➤ PUBLIC TOILETS | Inveraray Pier and Castle |
| ➤ CONTRIBUTOR | Ronald Turnbull |

## walk directions

**1** Follow the seafront past the Argyll Hotel and bear left towards **Inveraray Castle**. At the first junction, turn right past a football pitch with a standing stone. After the coach park on the left and the end wall of the castle on the right, the estate road on the left is signed 'Dun na Cuaiche Walk'. It passes a memorial to clansmen who were killed for religious reasons in 1685. Cross the stone-arched **Garden Bridge** to a junction.

**2** Turn right to a riverside track and follow it to a picnic table with a view back to the castle. A rough track runs up left, but turn off instead on to a small path just to right of this, beside a stone gatepost. It climbs quite steeply through an area where attempts are currently being made to eradicate rhododendron (but the rhodies are winning).

**3** At a green track above, turn left, slightly downhill, for 50yds (46m). Steps on the right lead up to a terraced path that goes slightly downhill around the hillside for ¼ mile (400m). Turn sharp right up a steep path with a rope handrail. This works its way back around the hill, passing below a small crag. Where it crosses a couple of open screes, there are fine views out to the right over Inveraray. At a path junction, turn left, following a waymarker pole up through woods. As the slope eases, the path crosses a grassy clearing to meet a wider one. Turn left, in zig-zags, to reach the summit of **Dun na Cuaiche**. The tower at the top is placed so it can be seen from below, but also offers outstanding views.

**4** Return down the path to the clearing, but this time keep ahead. The path, rather muddy, bends left then enters the plantation and becomes a clear track. It passes between two dry-stone pillars where a wall crosses, turns back sharp left, and passes between two more pillars lower down the same wall. Continue down the track, ignoring side-tracks on the left, to a **lime kiln** on the right.

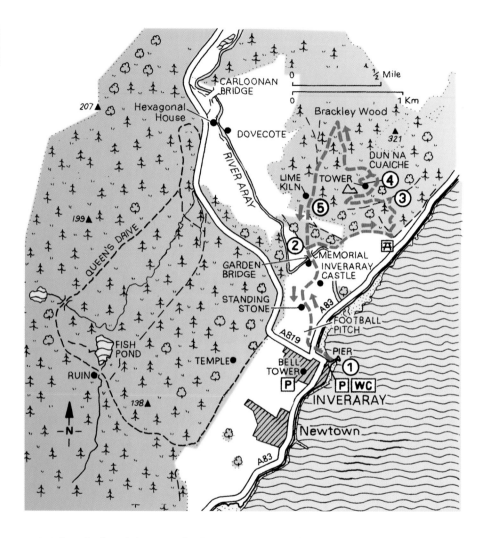

**5** Below the lime kiln, a gate leads out into an open field. Cross this diagonally left, going straight over a track to a kissing gate beyond. This leads into a wood of sycamores, and bluebells if you're here in May. The path runs down to the track junction before the **Garden Bridge** (Point ②). Return along the castle driveway to **Inveraray**.

*A rugged waterfall walk into the hidden hollow in Coire Gabhail, where the MacDonalds hid their stolen cows.*

# Into the Lost Valley

ABOVE: *Buachaille Etive Beag reflected in Lochan na Fola, Glen Coe*

The romantically named Lost Valley is 'Coire Gabhail' in Gaelic, the Corrie of Booty. Here, during the centuries leading up to the Glen Coe massacre of 1692, the MacDonalds hid their stolen cattle when the owners came storming in over the Moor of Rannoch with torch and claymore. It seems incredible that even the sure-footed black cattle of the clans could have been persuaded up the slope to Coire Gabhail. The corrie entrance is blocked by two old landslides from the face of Gearr Aonach, the middle hill of Glen Coe's Three Sisters. Stream shingle, backing up behind the obstruction, forms the smooth valley floor.

## Noble Profession of Cattle Thief

The economic system of Highland Scotland, until the end of the clans in 1745, was based on the keeping and the stealing of cattle. It was an unsettled and dangerous lifestyle, and its artform was the verse of the bard, who celebrated the most ingenious or violent acts of thievery and kept track of feuds.

## Raiders of Glen Coe

The clan, gathered under its chieftain, was an organisation for protecting its own glen and for stealing from its neighbours. The MacDonalds of Glen Coe were particularly good at it. They raided right across the country, passing the fringes of the Cairngorms to steal from the fertile lands of Aberdeenshire and Moray. In 1689, when Campbell of Glen Lyon was a guest in the house of MacIan, chief of Glen Coe, his cold blue eyes may have dwelt on a particular cooking pot. Twice in the previous ten years, MacIan had come raiding into Glen Lyon, dishonoured the women by cutting off their hair and, on the second occasion, stolen that pot from Campbell's own mother.

## The Massacre

By the late 1600s, the clan and the claymore were being replaced by a legal system backed by the central government and its army. But because they were so good at cattle thieving, the MacDonalds of Glen Coe continued the practice long after everyone else had, reluctantly, started to move into the modern world of cash. As a result, the government decided to make an example of them.

On a cold February day, a squad of soldiers arrived in the valley. Traditional hospitality meant that even its leader Glen Lyon, a Campbell and an enemy, was welcomed into the house of MacDonald. Five nights later, at a given signal, the soldiers rose from their beds and started murdering their hosts. The Glen Coe Massacre was either incompetent or mercifully half-hearted. Of the valley's population of 300, just 40 were killed, with the remainder escaping through the snow to the Lost Valley and the other high corries.

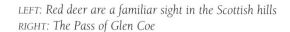

*LEFT: Red deer are a familiar sight in the Scottish hills*
*RIGHT: The Pass of Glen Coe*

## walk directions

1 From the uphill corner of the car park, a faint path slants down to the old road, which is now a well-used track. Head up-valley for about 650yds (594m). With the old road continuing as a green track ahead, your path now bends down to the right. It has been rebuilt, with the bog problem solved by scraping down to the bedrock. The path reaches the gorge where the **River Coe** runs in a geological dyke of softer rock. Descend on a steep wooden step ladder, to cross a spectacular footbridge.

2 The ascent out of the gorge is on a bare rock staircase. Above, the path runs through regenerating birch wood, which can be very wet on the legs; sheep and deer have been excluded from the wood with a temporary fence. Emerge over this by a high ladder stile. The path, rebuilt in places, runs uphill for 60yds (55m). Here it bends left; an inconspicuous alternative path continues uphill, which can be used to bypass the narrow path of the main route.

3 The main route contours into the gorge of the **Allt Coire Gabhail**. It is narrow with steep drops below. Where there is an alternative of rock slabs and a narrow path just below, the slabs are more secure. You will hear waterfalls, then two fine ones come into view ahead. After passing these, continue between boulders to where the main path bends left to cross the stream below a boulder the size of a small house. (A small path runs on up to right of the stream, but leads nowhere useful.) The river here is wide and fairly shallow. Five or six stepping stones usually allow dry crossing. If the water is above the stones, then it's safer to wade alongside them; if the water is more than knee-deep the crossing should not be attempted.

4 A well-built path continues uphill, now with the stream on its right. After 100yds (91m), a lump of rock blocks the way. The path follows a slanting ramp up its right-hand side. It continues uphill, still rebuilt in places, passing

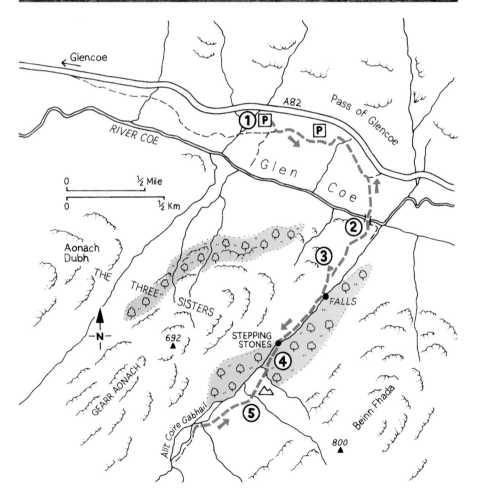

above the boulder pile that blocks the valley, the result of two large rockfalls from under Gearr Aonach opposite. At the top of the rockpile the path levels, giving a good view into the **Lost Valley**.

5 Drop gently to the valley's gravel floor. The stream vanishes into the gravel, to reappear below the boulder pile on the other side. Note where the path arrives at the gravel, as it becomes invisible at that point. Wander up the valley to where the stream vanishes, ¼ mile (400m) ahead. Anywhere beyond this point is more serious hillwalking than you have done up to now on this walk. Return to the path and follow it back to the start of the walk.

FAR LEFT: *Beech trees in Glen Coe wood*
LEFT: *Adnach Eagach Ridge, Glen Coe*

## walk information

| | |
|---|---|
| ➤ **DISTANCE** | 2¾ miles (4.4km) |
| ➤ **MINIMUM TIME** | 2hrs 15min |
| ➤ **ASCENT/GRADIENT** | 1,050ft (320m) ▲▲▲ |
| ➤ **LEVEL OF DIFFICULTY** | 🚶🚶 🚶🚶 🚶🚶 |
| ➤ **PATHS** | Rugged and stony, stream to wade through, 1 stile |
| ➤ **LANDSCAPE** | Crags and mountains |
| ➤ **SUGGESTED MAP** | OS Explorer 384 Glen Coe & Glen Etive |
| ➤ **START/FINISH** | Grid reference: NN 168569 |
| ➤ **DOG FRIENDLINESS** | Dogs must be reasonably fit and agile |
| ➤ **PARKING** | Lower of two roadside parking places opposite Gearr Aonach (middle one of Three Sisters) |
| ➤ **PUBLIC TOILETS** | Glencoe village |
| ➤ **CONTRIBUTOR** | Ronald Turnbull |

*A deeply wooded riverside leads from
the famous battlefield to Loch Faskally.*

# The Braes o' Killiecrankie

*'If ye'd hae been where I hae been
Ye wouldna been sae swanky o
If ye'd hae seen where I hae seen
On the braes o Killiecrankie o'*

The song commemorating the victory of the Battle of Killiecrankie in 1689 is still sung in tourist-packed pubs. In fact, both sides in the battle were Scottish. When James II was ousted from England in a bloodless coup in 1688, the Scots Parliament (the Estates) voted to replace him with William of Orange. The Stuarts had neglected and mismanaged Scotland, and had mounted a bloody persecution of the fundamentalist Protestants (Covenanters) of the Southern Uplands.

*ABOVE: A lone piper on the shores of
Loch Rannoch*
*RIGHT: The Pitlochry Hydro Hotel*

## 'Bluidy Clavers'

John Claverhouse, 'Bonnie Dundee', had earned the rather different nickname 'Bluidy Clavers' in those persecutions. He now raised a small army of Highlanders in support of King James. The Estates sent a larger army north under another Highlander, General Hugh Mackay, to sort things out. Dundee, outnumbered two to one, was urged to ambush Mackay in the Pass of Killiecrankie. He refused, on the grounds of chivalry. The path above the river was steep, muddy and wide enough for only two soldiers; a surprise attack on such difficult ground would give his broadsword-wielding Highlanders too great an advantage against Mackay's inexperienced troops. Thus, just one of the Lowlanders was picked off by an Atholl sharpshooter at the Trouper's Den (below today's visitor centre), and the battle actually took place on open ground, to the north of the pass.

## Claymore Victorious

Killiecrankie was the last time the claymore conquered the musket in open battle, and it was down to a deficiency in the musket. Some 900 of the 2,500 Highlanders were shot down as they charged, but then the troopers had to stop to fix their bayonets, which plugged into the muzzle of the musket. By this time the Highlanders were upon them, and they broke and fled. The battle had lasted just three minutes. Half of Mackay's army was killed, wounded, captured or drowned in the Garry. One escaped by leaping 18ft (5.5m) across the river; the 'Soldier's Leap' is near the start of the walk. The victory led nowhere, Bonnie Dundee died in the battle. A month later his army was defeated at Dunkeld, and 25 years later, when the Highlanders next brought their broadswords south for the Stuarts, the troopers had learnt to fix a bayonet.

*LEFT: The Pass of Killicrankie*

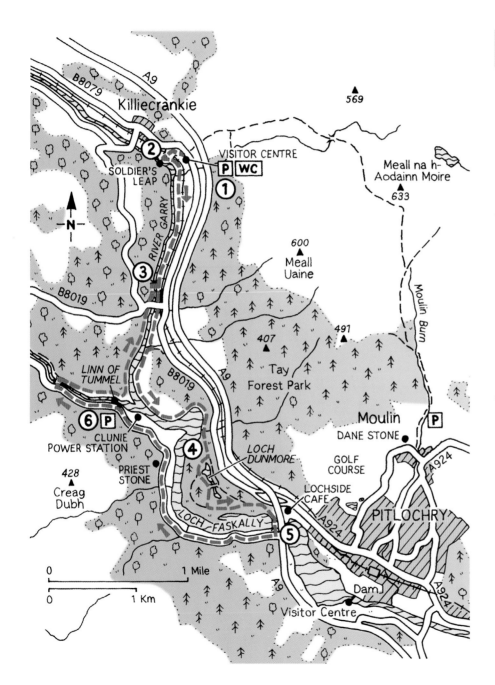

## walk directions

**1** Cross the front of the visitor centre to steps, signed 'Soldier's Leap', leading down into the wooded gorge. A footbridge crosses the waterfall of **Troopers' Den**. At the next junction, turn left ('Soldier's Leap'). Ten steps down, a spur path on the right leads to the viewpoint above the **Soldier's Leap**.

**2** Return to the main path, signed 'Linn of Tummel', which runs down to join the **River Garry** below the railway viaduct. After a mile (1.6km), it reaches a footbridge.

**3** Don't cross this footbridge, but continue ahead, signed 'Pitlochry', along the riverside under the tall South Garry road bridge. The path runs around a huge river pool to a tarred lane; turn right here. The lane leaves the lochside, then passes a track on the right, blocked by a vehicle barrier. Ignore this; shortly turn right at a signpost, 'Pitlochry'.

**4** Immediately bear left to pass along the right-hand side of **Loch Dunmore**, following red-top posts. A footbridge crosses the loch, but turn away from it, half right, on to a small path that becomes a dirt track. After 110yds (100m), it reaches a wider track. Turn left, with a white/yellow waymarker. After 220yds (201m) the track starts to climb; here the white/yellow markers indicate a smaller path on the right, which follows the lochside. Where it rejoins the wider path, bear right at a green waymarker and cross a footbridge to the **A9** road bridge.

**5** Cross **Loch Faskally** on the Clunie footbridge below the road's bridge and turn right, on to a quiet road around the loch. In 1 mile (1.6km), at the top of the grass bank on the left, is the **Priest Stone**. After the **Clunie power station**, you reach a car park on the left. Here a sign indicates a steep little path down to the **Linn of Tummel**.

6 Return to the road above for ½ mile (800m), to cross a grey suspension bridge on the right. Turn right, downstream, to pass above the **Linn**. A spur path back right returns to the falls at a lower level, but the main path continues along the riverside (signed 'Killiecrankie'). It bends left and goes down wooden steps to the **Garry**, then runs upstream and under the high road bridge. Take the side-path up on to the bridge for the view of the river, then return to follow the descending path signed 'Pitlochry via Faskally'. This runs down to the bridge, Point ③. Cross to the eastern bank of the river and return upstream to the start.

RIGHT: *Loch Faskally*

BELOW: *A marching tartan bagpipe band closing the Pitlochry Highland Games*

## walk information

| | |
| --- | --- |
| ➤ **DISTANCE** | 8¾ miles (14.1km) |
| ➤ **MINIMUM TIME** | 4hrs |
| ➤ **ASCENT/GRADIENT** | 492ft (150m) ▲ ▲ ▲ |
| ➤ **LEVEL OF DIFFICULTY** | 𝕩 𝕩 𝕩 |
| ➤ **PATHS** | Wide riverside paths, minor road, no stiles |
| ➤ **LANDSCAPE** | Oakwoods on banks of two rivers |
| ➤ **SUGGESTED MAP** | OS Explorer 386 Pitlochry & Loch Tummel |
| ➤ **START/FINISH** | Grid reference: NN 917626 |
| ➤ **DOG FRIENDLINESS** | Off leads on riverside paths |
| ➤ **PARKING** | Killiecrankie visitor centre |
| ➤ **PUBLIC TOILETS** | At start |
| ➤ **CONTRIBUTOR** | Ronald Turnbull |

*Classic rock climbing country below the A'Chioch and the Inaccessible Pinnacle.*

# Heart of the Cuillins

*ABOVE: The Cuillin Hills across Loch Scavaig from Elgol, Isle of Skye*

The Black Cuillin Hills, seen through Skye's moist Atlantic air, appear blue and under romantic sunset light almost purple. This land is like nowhere else, even in Scotland, for crag, boulder and jagged horizon.

## The Glory of Gabbro

The special quality of Skye is obvious to the eye, but even more so to the foot. The black rock grips the foot like velcro. This is gabbro, formed in the magma chamber of a volcano bigger than Kilimanjaro that stood here 50 million years ago. Skye's screes are the steepest, its crags the craggiest, and its ridges look out across the Hebrides and the Atlantic. For rock climbers and mountaineers, on the rare days when it isn't raining, this is paradise.

As you approach Point ④ on the upward journey, you are looking towards the buttress of Sron na Ciche. High on the face is a smooth, diamond-shaped slab and, at its right-hand corner, a famous rock-projection. It long went unnoticed, until a famous climber, Professor Norman Collie, spotted the shadow it casts across the slab in the afternoon. This is A'Chioch, 'the Beast'. Its flat top was the scene of a sword-fight in the film *Highlander*. The top is reached by a spectacular, but fairly straightforward climb.

## Behind Lagan

In the upper corrie, more famous bits of rock come into view. At the back right corner is the long scree called the Great Stone Shoot. It is strenuous and frustrating but not technically difficult, and it brings climbers up to the ridge just to the right of Skye's highest peak, Sgurr Alasdair. The skyline to left of the Stone Shoot is dominated by Sgurr Mhic Choinnich, with its near-vertical right profile. This step, 200ft (61m) high, can be avoided by a remarkable ledge that crosses below the summit, to emerge on the mountain's gentler left-hand ridge.

To the left again, you can just see the rock-prow of the so-called Inaccessible Pinnacle. This forms the summit of Skye's second highest peak, Sgurr Dearg. Its easiest route is very scary, but only moderately difficult and fairly accessible. It must be climbed by anyone wishing to complete the Munro summits, Scottish peaks over 3,000ft (914m), and on summer weekends there will be a queue of several hours at its foot.

*LEFT: The Cuillins rise beyond River Sligachan*
*RIGHT: View of the Cuillin Hills from Loch Brittle*

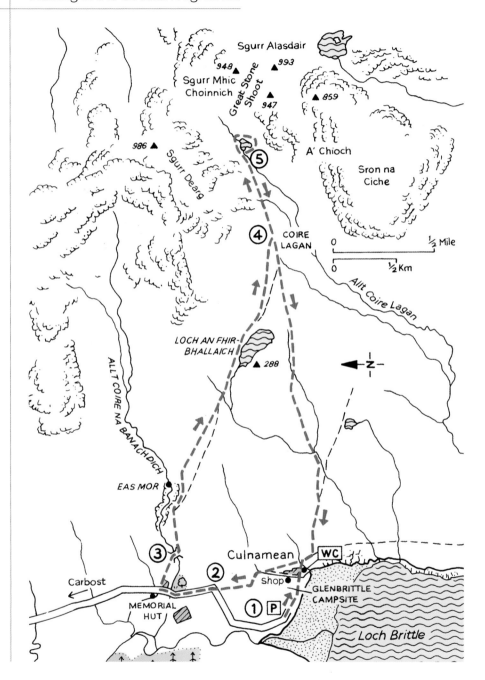

## walk information

| | |
|---|---|
| ➤ **DISTANCE** | 5¾ miles (9.2km) |
| ➤ **MINIMUM TIME** | 4hrs |
| ➤ **ASCENT/GRADIENT** | 1,900ft (580m) ▲▲▲ |
| ➤ **LEVEL OF DIFFICULTY** | 🚶🚶🚶 |
| ➤ **PATHS** | Mountain paths, one boggy and tough, 2 stiles |
| ➤ **LANDSCAPE** | Peaty slopes into spectacular crag hollow |
| ➤ **SUGGESTED MAP** | OS Explorer 411 Skye – Cuillin Hills |
| ➤ **START/FINISH** | Grid reference: NG 409206 |
| ➤ **DOG FRIENDLINESS** | Signs indicate necessity for leads in sheep country below corrie |
| ➤ **PARKING** | Walkers' pull-off before gate into Glenbrittle campsite |
| ➤ **PUBLIC TOILETS** | At campsite |
| ➤ **CONTRIBUTOR** | Ronald Turnbull |

## walk directions

**1** From the parking area, the track leads on through **Glenbrittle campsite** to a gate with a kissing gate. Pass to left of the toilet block to cross a stile. Turn left along a stony track just above, which runs gently downhill above the campsite, to rejoin the **Glenbrittle road**.

**2** Keep walking ahead to cross a bridge with the white **Memorial Hut** just ahead. On the right are some stone buchts (sheep-handling enclosures) and here a waymarked path heads uphill to reach a footbridge that crosses the **Allt Coire na Banachdich**.

**3** Cross the footbridge and head up to the right of the stream's deep ravine. Look out for a short side-path on the left for the best view of the waterfall at its head. Its Gaelic name, **Eas Mor**, means simply 'Big Waterfall'. Above, the path bears right, to slant up the hillside. This part of the path has never been built or repaired and is bog and boulder. It passes above **Loch an Fhir-bhallaich** and forks, with the left-hand and higher branch being drier but with loose eroded scree. It rounds a shoulder into the lower part of **Coire Lagan** and meets a much larger and better path.

4  Turn uphill on this path, until a belt of bare rock blocks the way into the upper corrie. This rock has been smoothed by a glacier into gently-rounded swells, known as 'boiler-plates'. A scree field runs up into the boiler-plate rocks. The best way keeps up the left edge, below a slab wall with a small waterslide, to the highest point of the scree. Head up left for a few steps on bare rock, then back right on ledges to an eroded scree above the boiler-plate obstruction. Look back down your upward route to note it for your return. The trodden way slants up to the right. With the main stream near by on the right, it goes up to the rim of the upper corrie.

5  The boiler-plate slabs at the lochan's outflow are an excellent place for picnics. Walking mainly on bare rock, it's easy to make a circuit of the lochan. For the return journey, retrace your steps to Point ④. Ignoring the right fork of the route you came up by, keep straight downhill on the main path. It runs straight down to the toilet block at **Glenbrittle campsite**.

*RIGHT: Bla Bheinn, Cuillin Hills, Skye*

*From a Victorian spa*
*through woodland to a*
*salmon-leaping waterfall.*

# The Falls of Rogie

Stand on the suspension bridge at Falls of Rogie between July and September, at a time when the river's fairly full, and you might catch a glimpse of the silver flash of a leaping salmon. It's a thrilling sight to see a 3ft (1m) long fish attempting to swim up against the force of the water. Eventually it'll make it, or else discover the easy way round – the fish ladder carved out of the rock on the right-hand side. If you'd been here 200 years ago, that single salmon would have been a dozen or even a hundred. During the autumn run, the falls must have appeared almost to flow in reverse, an upstream current of flashing fish.

LEFT: *Overlooking Strathpeffer from*
*Hector Macdonald monument*

## The Rise and Fall of the Salmon

Salmon was once food for the taking, like blackberries today. You went down to the river and took as many as you thought you could eat. Smoked above the peat fire of the black houses, it was a staple food through the winter. Farm workers even used their industrial muscle to demand that they shouldn't be obliged to eat salmon more than three times a week.

Today, however, this majestic fish is steadily heading towards extinction. In the last ten years, the catch in Scotland's rivers has shrunk from 1,200 tons to 200. The main reason has been netting in the estuaries, and in their feeding grounds around the Arctic pack ice. Angling clubs have bought up and discontinued estuary netting rights. The international community still squabbles on about the Arctic drift nets, and now a new danger to wild fish is posed by parasites and disease leaking out of the sea cages of Scotland's 340 fish farms.

Egg, fry, alevin, parr, smolt, salmon, kelt – these are the seven ages of the salmon's extraordinary life. For one or two years it behaves like a trout, hanging in the still water behind a boulder and waiting for food to float by. But then in one of nature's changes, as striking in its way as a caterpillar becoming a butterfly or a tadpole becoming a frog, its scales become silver and it turns downstream, totally altering its body chemistry for life in the salt water. Its new name of 'smolt' is probably a reference to silver poured from the furnace. Four or five years later, now called a salmon, it returns. We don't know how it navigates from Greenland back to the Cromarty Firth. Once back in Scotland, it identifies the outflow of the Conon by the taste of the water and works its way upstream, taking all the correct turnings to the patch of gravel where it was once an egg and an alevin.

*BELOW: Strathpeffer from the Knock Farril walk*

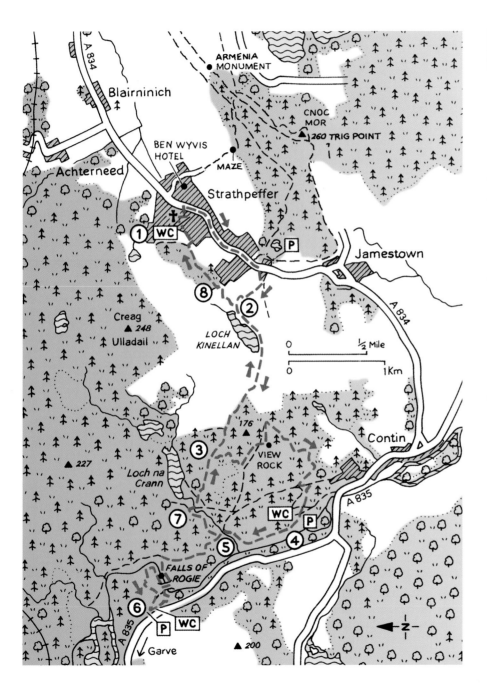

## walk directions

1 Head along the main road towards **Contin**. When you reach the edge of the town, turn right at a signpost for Garve then, at a bend in the lane, turn left, following another signpost.

2 Pass round to the left of **Loch Kinellan**, then keep ahead up a faint path through gorse to the corner of a plantation. Here you join a larger track leading into the forest. After another ¼ mile (400m), it reaches a signpost.

3 Turn left for **View Rock** on a good path with green waymarkers. At View Rock, a side-path diverts to the right for the viewpoint. After a steep descent, ignore a green path turning off to the left and follow green waymarkers downhill. At a forest road turn left, then back right for 60yds (55m) to a path on the left. It crosses another forest road to a car park.

4 At the end of the car park you'll pick up a wide path signed 'River Walk'. After a stream culvert, the main path bends up to the right, past a waymark with a roe deer head to a forest road. Turn left, signposted 'Garve', and in another 80yds (73m) bear left, heading slightly downhill.

5 Go on for 600yds (549m), when a small track on the left is signed 'Falls of Rogie'. At its foot, cross a spectacular footbridge below the falls and turn right, upstream. The path has green waymarkers and after ¼ mile (400m) bends left, away from the river. It crosses rocky ground to a junction. Turn up right, to a car park.

6 Leave the car park through a wooden arch and follow green waymarkers back to the bridge. Retrace the outward route to Point ⑤ and turn sharp left up another forest road. It leads uphill to a four-way junction.

## walk information

| | |
|---|---|
| ➤ **DISTANCE** | 10 miles (16.1km) |
| ➤ **MINIMUM TIME** | 5hrs |
| ➤ **ASCENT/GRADIENT** | 1,200ft (365m) ▲ ▲ ▲ |
| ➤ **LEVEL OF DIFFICULTY** | 🚶 🚶 🚶 |
| ➤ **PATHS** | Waymarked paths and track, no stiles |
| ➤ **LANDSCAPE** | Plantation, wild forest and riverside |
| ➤ **SUGGESTED MAP** | OS Explorer 437 Ben Wyvis & Strathpeffer |
| ➤ **START/FINISH** | Grid reference: NH 483582 |
| ➤ **DOG FRIENDLINESS** | On lead for section past Loch Kinellan |
| ➤ **PARKING** | Main square, Strathpeffer |
| ➤ **PUBLIC TOILETS** | At start, Contin (Point 4) and Falls of Rogie car parks |
| ➤ **CONTRIBUTOR** | Ronald Turnbull |

7 Turn right on a smaller track to pass between obstructing boulders, then left on a rutted path to rejoin the same track higher up. After 600yds (549m), it reaches the signpost at Point ③. Keep ahead and retrace the outward route to Point ②. Turn left on the tarred lane, which becomes a track. Keep ahead towards a house, but before it, turn left through a kissing gate, with a second one beyond leading into a plantation with a signpost for Strathpeffer.

8 Follow the main track ahead until you see **Strathpeffer** down on the right. At the next junction, bear right down the wood edge and turn right into the town. The street on the left leads past a church with a square steeple, where you turn down right to the main square.

RIGHT: *The Eagle Stone, north of Strathpeffer*

*Following cattle thieves and drovers to the lochan used by the fairies for their laundry.*

# The Pass of Ryvoan and the Thieves' Road

ABOVE: *Loch Morlich, Aviemore*

The Pass of Ryvoan has all the atmosphere of a classic Cairngorm through-route. It's a scaled down version of the famous and fearsome Lairig Ghru that cuts through the Cairngorm range southwards from Aviemore. You pass from the shelter of the forest to a green lochan, trapped between two high and stony mountainsides. Once through the narrow gap, you feel as if you're in a different country. Here you will find wide moors and a ring of peaks around the horizon.

## Thieving Ways

Ryvoan marked the exit of the Thieves' Road that ran out of Rannoch and Lochaber by secret ways through the Rothiemurchus Forest. The MacDonalds of Glen Coe used to come cattle raiding here in the 17th century, as did Clan Cameron from Loch Eil near Fort William. Once through the pass, they could take their pick from the rich lands of Moray and Aberdeenshire.

In more settled times, the raiding chieftains became landlords, and their rents were paid in the small black cattle of the glens. Every autumn, the drove herds assembled for their long walk to the cattle markets of Falkirk, Perth and northern England.

*BELOW, RIGHT AND PAGE 71: Loch Morlich, with the Cairngorms in the background*

## The Old Drove Road

The drovers used the same road as their thieving grandfathers, but once through the pass they turned sharp right across the flank of the mountain. The Lairig an Lui, the Pass of the Calves, crosses the dangerous ford of the Avon and runs down Glen Derry to Braemar. It's 30 miles (48km) to the next good grazing and shelter from the rain – two full days for the drove. Overnight, the cattle would snatch some grazing from the rough grasses, while the drovers cooked their oatmeal and potatoes, before rolling themselves in their woollen plaids on a bed of heather. As late as 1859, Queen Victoria found the Lairig path torn up by hooves and scented with fresh cow pats.

## The Sith and Others

Lochan Uaine means 'Green Loch'. Some say the green colour is caused by flecks of mica. Others claim that it's where the fairies wash their green garments. The Highland fairies, the Sith (pronounced 'Shee'), don't dance around with magic wands and grant you three wishes. They are touchy and vengeful, and if you meet one it is best to address him very politely in good Gaelic. Precautions you can take are to avoid wearing green, which is known to annoy them, and never to address your friends by name while still under the trees.

The Bodach Lamh-dearg is a spectre who appears wrapped in a grey plaid with one bloodstained hand, challenging passers-by to a fight and leaving their bodies for the foxes. Big Donald, the King of the Fairies, lived beside Loch Morlich. While wolves and bears may one day return to the forest, we should be more alarmed about the return of the Sith.

## walk directions

1 Head upstream on a sandy track to the left of the river. Interpretation signs explain the flowers of the forest you may come across, many of which are ferns and mosses. After 550yds (503m), turn left on a wide, smooth path with blue/yellow waymarkers. Ahead is a gate into **Glenmore Lodge** rifle range; here the path bends right, to a wide gravel track.

2 Turn right, away from Glenmore Lodge, to cross a concrete bridge into the **Caledonian Reserve**. Immediately keep ahead on a smaller track (marked by a blue waymarker), as the main one bends right. The track narrows as it heads into the **Pass of Ryvoan** between steep, wooded slopes of pine, birch and scree. At a sign that warns of the end of waymarking, a path turns left, with a blue waymarker,

## walk information

| | |
|---|---|
| ➤ **DISTANCE** | 5 miles (8km) |
| ➤ **MINIMUM TIME** | 2hrs 15min |
| ➤ **ASCENT/GRADIENT** | 400ft (122m) ▲▲🔺 |
| ➤ **LEVEL OF DIFFICULTY** | 🚶🚶🚶 |
| ➤ **PATHS** | Smooth tracks, one steep ascent, no stiles |
| ➤ **LANDSCAPE** | Views over Rothiemurchus Forest to Cairngorms |
| ➤ **SUGGESTED MAP** | OS Explorer 403 Cairn Gorm & Aviemore |
| ➤ **START/FINISH** | Grid reference: NH 980095 |
| ➤ **DOG FRIENDLINESS** | Off leads but under close control |
| ➤ **PARKING** | Bridge just south of Glenmore village |
| ➤ **PUBLIC TOILETS** | Glenmore village |
| ➤ **CONTRIBUTOR** | Ronald Turnbull |

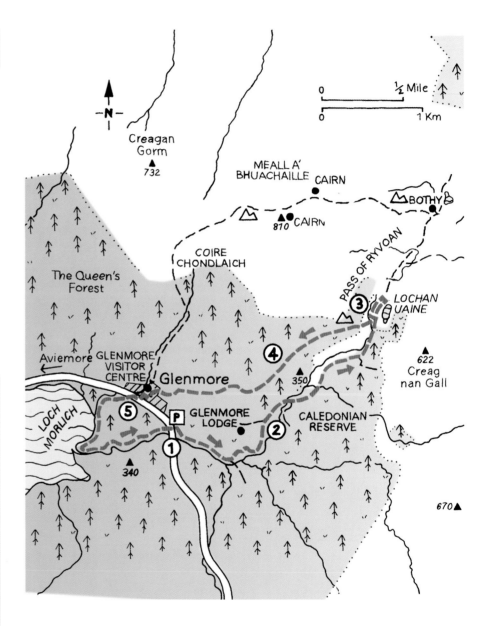

which you take in a moment. Just beyond this, steps on the right lead down to **Lochan Uaine**. Walk round to the left of the water, on the beach. At the head of the loch, a small path leads back up to the track. Turn sharp left, back to the junction already visited; now turn off to the right on to the narrower path with the blue waymarker.

3 This small path crosses some duckboard and heads back down the valley. Very soon it starts to climb steeply to the right, up rough stone steps. When it levels off, the going is easier, although it's still narrow with tree roots. The path reaches a forest road at a bench and a waymarker.

4 Continue to the left along the track. After a clear-felled area with views, the track re-enters trees and slopes downhill into Glenmore village. Just above the main road turn right, through a green barrier, to reach **Glenmore Visitor Centre**. Pass through its car park to the main road.

5 Cross to **Glenmore shop**, with its café. Behind a red post-box, steps lead down to the campsite. Pass along its right-hand edge to a wide, smooth path into birch woods (blue/brown waymarkers). Head left across a footbridge to the shore of **Loch Morlich** and follow the shore's sandy beaches (or paths in the woods on the left) until another river blocks the way. Turn left along the riverbank. Ignore a footbridge, but continue on the wide path (following brown/blue waymarkers) with the river on your right. Where the path divides, the smaller branch, with blue waymarkers, continues beside the river through broom bushes to the car park at the start of the walk.

*A circuit of Iona to the marble quarry and the saint's landing place in Coracle Bay.*

# The Holy Island of St Columba

I n the early summer of AD 563, a middle-aged cleric crossed over from Ireland with twelve companions and the intention of setting up a monastic community on the remote and windswept island of Iona. This walk takes you to the bay where he landed and explores the island that St Columba called home.

ABOVE: *Abbey cloisters, Iona*
RIGHT: *Rocky shoreline of Iona*

## Flight of the Dove

Columba (in Gaelic, Colum Cille, the Dove of the Church) did not intend to bring Christianity to a new country, indeed he had left his native Ireland under a cloud. It had started with a dispute over copyright: Columba had secretly copied a psalter owned by St Finnian of Clonard, and Finnian had claimed ownership of the copy. The dispute became more complicated when a young prince accidentally killed an opponent during a game of Irish hockey and claimed sanctuary with Columba. A battle followed, for which Columba felt responsible. It was in penance for these events that he accepted 'white martyrdom', or perpetual exile.

*BELOW: Baile Mor, Iona*

## Irish Poetry

At the centre of Columba's settlement on Iona was a church of oak logs and thatch and, around it, huts for the individual monks. Columba himself slept on the bedrock with a stone for a pillow. Larger huts of wattle were used as the dining hall, guest house, library and writing room. The monks' lives consisted of prayer, simple farming and study, and here Columba composed poetry in Latin and Irish.

## Celtic Calendar Calculations

Columba's Celtic Christianity spread from Iona across Scotland, and led to the Northumbrian foundation of Lindisfarne, with its rich tradition of illustrated documents, such as the Lindisfarne Gospel. Here, it came into contact with the Roman-style Christianity of continental Europe, brought to England by Augustine in AD 597. While the outward dispute was on the correct hairstyle for monks and the way to calculate the date of Easter, it seems that the Celtic Christianity was more personal and mystical, the Roman more authoritarian. The Roman version eventually dominated, but the Celtic was never suppressed. Columba, never officially canonised as a saint, is still venerated in Scotland and Ireland.

## Iona Today

Columba's church vanished beneath a later Benedictine abbey, itself heavily restored in the 19th century. However the spirit of Columba still dominates the island. From the low hill called Dun I, on the day of his death, he blessed the island and community. The monks grew kale and oats at the machars (coastal lowlands) of Bay at the Back of the Ocean (Camus Cuil an t-Saimh), over what is today the golf course. At the southern tip of the island is Coracle Bay, traditionally named as the saint's landing place.

'That man is little to be envied, whose patriotism would not gain force upon the plain of Marathon, or whose piety would not grow warmer among the ruins of Iona,' said the renowned English writer and critic Samuel Johnson, who visited the island in 1773. Today's Iona Foundation is ecumenical – tied to no single denomination of

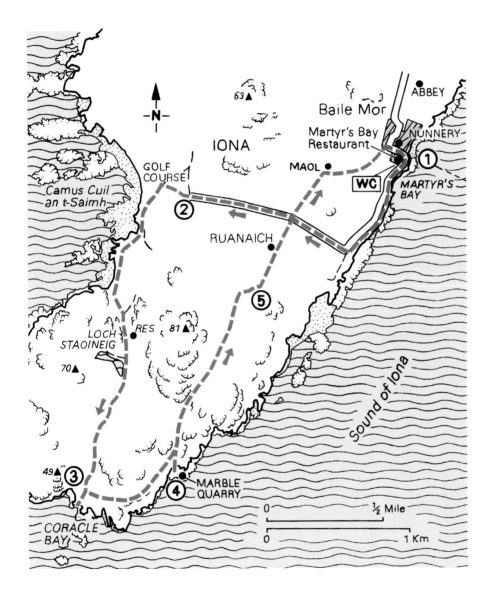

**1** Ferries cross to Iona about every hour. Once on the island, take the tarred road on the left, passing **Martyr's Bay**. After a second larger bay, rejoin the road as it bends right. Follow the road across the island to a gate on to the Iona golf course (dogs on leads).

**2** Take the sandy track ahead, then bear left past a small cairn to the shore. Turn left along the shore to a large beach. At its end, bear left up a narrow valley. After 100yds (91m), you pass a small concrete hut to join a stony track. It passes a fenced reservoir and drops to the corner of **Loch Staoineig**. Walk along to the left of the lochan on a path, improved in places, that runs gently down to **Coracle Bay**. You cross to the left of an area that shows the furrows of lazybed cultivation – fields drained to improve crop yields – and reach the shore just to the left of a rocky knoll.

## walk information

| | |
|---|---|
| ➤ **DISTANCE** | 5¼ miles (8.4km) |
| ➤ **MINIMUM TIME** | 3hrs 30min |
| ➤ **ASCENT/GRADIENT** | 650ft (198m) ▲▲ ▲ ▲ |
| ➤ **LEVEL OF DIFFICULTY** | 👫 👫 👫 |
| ➤ **PATHS** | Tracks, sandy paths, some rugged rock and heather |
| ➤ **LANDSCAPE** | Bare gneiss rock and Atlantic Ocean |
| ➤ **SUGGESTED MAP** | OS Explorer 373 Iona, Staffa & Ross of Mull |
| ➤ **START/FINISH** | Grid reference: NM 286240 |
| ➤ **DOG FRIENDLINESS** | On leads near sheep and across golf course |
| ➤ **PARKING** | Ferry terminal at Fionnphort on Mull |
| ➤ **PUBLIC TOILETS** | Beside Martyr's Bay Bar |
| ➤ **CONTRIBUTOR** | Ronald Turnbull |

Christianity – and has restored the buildings within a tradition of simple craftsmanship and prayer. The grave of John Smith, Labour leader in the 1990s, lies in the north east extension of the burial ground.

3 The route ahead is pathless and hard. If your ferry leaves in two hours time or earlier, return by the outward route and leave the marble quarries for another visit. Otherwise, return inland for 200yds (183m) and bear right into a little grassy valley. After 100yds (91m), go through a broken wall and bear slightly left, past another inlet on the right. Cross heather to the eastern shoreline of the island. Bear left, above the small sea cliff, for ¼ mile (400m). Turn sharp right into a little valley, descending to the remnants of the **marble quarry**.

4 Turn inland, back up the valley to its head. Pass the low walls of two ruined cottages and continue in the same direction for about 200yds (183m), to a fence corner. Keep the fence on your left, picking a way through heather, rock and bog on sheep paths. Dun I, with its cairn, appears ahead – aim directly for it to reach the edge of fields, where a fence runs across ahead. Turn right along it to reach a small iron gate.

5 This leads to a track that passes **Ruanaich farm** to the tarred road of the outward walk. Cross into a farm track, which bends to the right at **Maol**. It reaches **Baile Mor** (the Iona village) at the ruined nunnery. Just ahead is the abbey with its squat square tower, or turn right directly to the ferry pier.

*RIGHT: Ruins of Iona's priory building*

*A pleasant walk around Loch Kernsary and down the Ewe – the country's shortest river.*

# Into Scotland's Great Wilderness

*ABOVE: Gairloch village*

As you walk inland from Poolewe, you're entering one of the largest empty areas in Britain. Turn left instead of right at Kernsary farm, and you can walk for two full days before you reach a road.

## Great Wilderness

On the slight rise before Loch Kernsary, you get a surprise view right into the heart of this mountain wonderland. At the back of the view is A'Mhaighdean, the Maiden, Scotland's most remote mountain. It takes half a day's walk to get to this hill from anywhere. That walk will be along the edges of long dark lochs and under some very large crags. Beinn Lair has a quartzite cliff with an evil north-face gleam that's 3 miles (4.8km) wide, as big as the north face of Ben Nevis, but a whole lot less visited.

Behind A'Mhaighdean is An Teallach, called the Forge because of the cloudy vapours that stream across its semicircular ridge – imagine plunging a red hot sword into a water bucket. That ridge has great lumpy towers to scramble round, 3ft-wide (1m) ridges to walk along and an edge that if you fall off it will take about four seconds before you land on anything at all.

## The Letterewe Accord

All this belongs to a gentleman from Holland called Paul van Vlissingen. In 1993, he signed an agreement with the Mountaineering Council of Scotland that first set out the principle of responsible access for all. Deer stalking restrictions would be only on days when deer stalking was actually taking place – a step forward when walkers were sometimes threatened with high-velocity rifle fire from August to February. The estate also undertook not to build any new landrover tracks. As a result, business here is carried out on foot, by boat and by pony. This Letterewe Accord has become the foundation of the new century's access legislation.

*LEFT: An array of autumnal colours in Gairloch*

| walk information | |
|---|---|
| ➤ **DISTANCE** | 6½ miles (10.4km) |
| ➤ **MINIMUM TIME** | 2hrs 45min |
| ➤ **ASCENT/GRADIENT** | 250ft (76m) ▲▲▲ |
| ➤ **LEVEL OF DIFFICULTY** | 🚶🚶🚶 |
| ➤ **PATHS** | Mostly good, but one short, rough, wet section, 3 stiles |
| ➤ **LANDSCAPE** | Moorland and loch side |
| ➤ **SUGGESTED MAP** | OS Explorer 434 Gairloch & Loch Ewe |
| ➤ **START/FINISH** | Grid reference: NG 857808 |
| ➤ **DOG FRIENDLINESS** | Close control on moorland and tracks carrying estate traffic |
| ➤ **PARKING** | In Poolewe, just up B8057 side street |
| ➤ **PUBLIC TOILETS** | At start |
| ➤ **CONTRIBUTOR** | Ronald Turnbull |

## Rights of Way

The paths used on this walk are, as it happens, established rights of way. Even so, you'll notice a sudden change about halfway along the side of Loch Kernsary. The first part of the path has been rebuilt by the National Trust for Scotland, using their members' annual subscriptions. One new member pays for about 2ft (60cm) of path. At the edge of their land the repairs stop, mid-bog.

In Scotland, no one is obliged to build or maintain footpaths. The surprising thing, if you walk all 50 of these walks, is how many people are doing it anyway. Paths in this book are looked after by charities, such as the John Muir Trust, by Scottish Natural Heritage and Forest Enterprise, by private landowners in Argyll and Atholl, by regional and community councils and by groups of ordinary walkers.

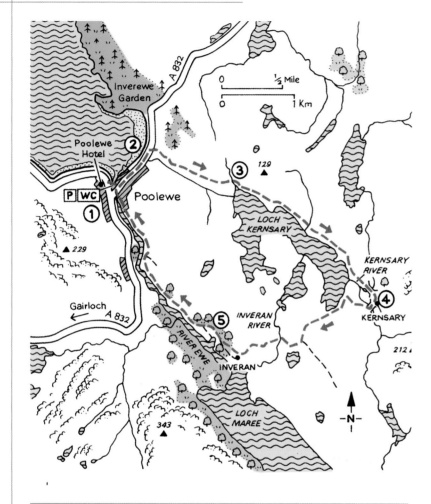

## walk directions

**1** A kissing gate beside the public toilets leads to a path that crosses the **Marie Curie Field of Hope** to the main road. Turn left to cross the bridge over the **River Ewe** and then head all the way through the village. At the 40mph derestriction sign, there's a white cottage on the right. Beside it, a tarred trackway has a Scottish Rights of Way Society signpost for Kernsary.

**2** Follow the track over a cattle grid to a new track that forks off to the left. After 50yds (46m), keep ahead on a path with a wall on its left. It passes through a kissing gate into **Cnoc na Lise**, the Garden Hill. This has been replanted as a community wood with oak and birch trees. Another kissing gate leads out of the young wood. The good, reconstructed path runs over some bare sandstone slabs and under a low-voltage power line. It crosses a low spur to a fine view of Loch Kernsary and the remote, steep-sided hills of the Great Wilderness, then goes over a stream to the loch side.

**3** The path follows the left-hand shore of the loch, passing through patches of birch scrub. About half-way along the loch, it suddenly deteriorates, becoming a braided trod of boulder and bog. From a stile at the loch head, slant to the left down a meadow to find a footbridge under an oak tree. Head up, with a fence on your right, to join a track beside **Kernsary farm**.

**4** Turn right, through a gate. Follow the track past the farm, to a culvert crossing of the **Kernsary River**. This becomes a ford only after heavy rain. If needed, you will find a footbridge 70yds (64m) upstream. After crossing, turn right on a smooth track. The new track bears left, away from Loch Kernsary towards the hollow containing Loch Maree. After the bridge over the **Inveran River** is a gate with a ladder stile. Signs welcoming responsible walkers (and even cyclists) reflect the principles of the Letterewe Accord. Soon come the first views of Loch Maree. The driveway of **Inveran house** joins from the left and the track starts being tarred.

**5** At a sign, 'Blind Corners', a green track on the left leads down to the point where the narrow loch imperceptibly becomes a wide river. Return to the main track and follow it above and then beside the **River Ewe**. It reaches **Poolewe** just beside the bridge.

*RIGHT: The shores of Gairloch village*

*A walk above Loch Torridon in the footsteps of the fairy folk – the legendary duine sithe.*

# Following the Diabaig Coast Path

ew Year's Eve in Wester Ross is a time when old songs are sung, whisky is drunk (not all of it approved by the exciseman either) and tales are told in both English and Gaelic. Over the years these stories mature and grow, and also change location, so that the tailor who lost his hump to the fairies lived not only in Scotland, but in Ireland and even Italy. Today it is categorised as 'folktale type 503'.

*ABOVE: An Otter in the Kingcraig Wildlife Park*
*RIGHT: Looking across Loch Torridon towards Beinn Alligin*

ABOVE: *View north to Liathach, overlooking the lakes and Torridon mountains*

## Fairy Tales and Ghosts

Many of the tales told in Alligin take place in the knolly, obviously magical ground on the way to Diabaig. One story concerns two men of the village, who were bringing whisky for the New Year from Gairloch by way of the coast path. They heard wonderful music and came upon a cave in the hill where the fairy people had started their Hogmanay celebrations a few hours early. Fascinated, the man with the keg crept closer and closer until he was actually inside, whereupon the cave closed up and disappeared. A year later the other man came back, found the cave open again and managed to drag his friend out across the threshold. The friend thought he'd been in there only a few minutes, but of the whisky he carried there was no trace.

At the top of the hill road is tiny Lochan Dearg, and here there is a ghost that appears only to people bearing his own name, Murdo Mackenzie. The kilted spirit, one of the Mackenzies of Gairloch, was slain by a Torridon MacDonald and buried somewhere near by.

## Horse Tale

Loch Diabaigas Airde (Point 2) is haunted by the water spirit called the kelpie. This appears as a magnificent white horse, but if you mount it, the horse gallops rapidly into the loch and you're never seen again. That is, unless you just happen to have a bridle that's made of pure silver to tame it. Another kelpie lives in the Lochan Toll nam Beiste, the Lochan of the Beast Hole, at the back of Beinn Alligin.

## How to Protect Yourself from the Duine Sithe

Be polite, but don't accept food from them. At best it'll be cow dung, at worst it'll enslave you for ever. Carry iron, oatmeal or a groundsel root for protection, and a cry of 'am monadh oirbh, a' bheistein' ('back to the hill, you wee beastie') is effective. Approaching Alligin Shuas, walk carefully past Cnoc nan Sithe, the Fairy Knoll. Fairy music has been heard above the gorge of the Alligin burn.

## walk information

| | |
|---|---|
| ➤ **DISTANCE** | 9½ miles (15.3km) |
| ➤ **MINIMUM TIME** | 6hrs |
| ➤ **ASCENT/GRADIENT** | 1,805ft (550m) ▲▲▲ |
| ➤ **LEVEL OF DIFFICULTY** | 🚶🚶 🚶🚶 🚶🚶 |
| ➤ **PATHS** | Narrow, rough and wet in places, no stiles |
| ➤ **LANDSCAPE** | Rocky knolls and small lochans |
| ➤ **SUGGESTED MAP** | OS Explorer 433 Torridon – Beinn Eighe & Liathach |
| ➤ **START/FINISH** | Grid reference: NG 840575 |
| ➤ **DOG FRIENDLINESS** | On lead passing Alligin Shuas; close control near sheep |
| ➤ **PARKING** | Informal camp and caravan site above Inveralligin |
| ➤ **PUBLIC TOILETS** | None on route or near by |
| ➤ **CONTRIBUTOR** | Ronald Turnbull |

## walk directions

**1** Follow the road right, past the village green and over the **Abhainn Alligin**. A path leads along the shoreline for 100yds (91m), then makes its way up right, among sandstone outcrops. Bear left under a power line to join the corner of a tarmac driveway. Keep ahead to **Alligin Shuas**.

**2** Turn up the road and then left, on the road for **Diabaig**. As the road steepens, you can take a path ahead, rejoining the road as it crosses a high pass and runs down past two lochs – Loch Diabaigas Airde and Loch a'Mhullaich – which are linked.

**3** Turn off left, crossing the outflow of **Loch a'Mhullaich** on a footbridge. A clear path leads out along the high wall of a stream valley, then zig-zags down a spur, aiming for a grey

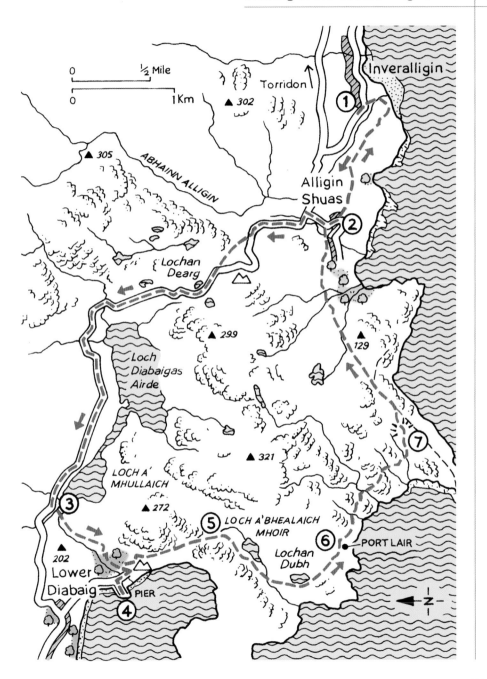

ABOVE: *Torridon village*

gate. Go down through woods to a white house, **No 1 Diabaig**. Turn right to reach the old stone pier.

4 Return up the path you just came down, to pass a stone shed. Here a sign indicates a turn to the right, under an outcrop and between boulders. The path heads up to a small rock step with an arrow mark and a convenient tree root which you can use to hold on to. It then leads up to a gate in a fence and zig-zags into an open gully with a large crag on the right. At the top of this, it turns right along a shelf, with still more crag above. The path slants gently down along the foot of another crag, then up to a col.

5 From here the path is small but clear. It bends right to **Loch a' Bhealaich Mhoir** and then turns left below it to reach yet another small loch. Follow its stream down towards the cottage of **Port Lair**.

6 Pass above the house, then slant gradually up away from the sea. The path crosses the head of a bracken valley with a ruined croft house, into a bleak knolly area out of sight of the sea. Cross two branches of a stream and go up to a cairn which marks where the path bears left up the spur. It now contours across a heathery meadow among the knolls, at the end of which it climbs pink rocks over a final spur. Here there is a good view up Loch Torridon to Liathach for the first time.

7 The path descends slightly to cross a high, steep slope of heather. Near the end of this slope, the path forks. Take the upper branch, to go through a wide col. The rather boggy path heads down towards **Alligin Shuas**. From a gate above the village, a faint path runs down in the direction of a distant green shed. It descends through a wood, then contours just above the village to reach the road above Point ②. Retrace your steps to the start of the walk.

*Through crofting country and*
*peat moors to a 1,000ft*
*(305m) sea cliff.*

# Waterstein Head

*ABOVE: Drystone dyke*

After the defeat of Bonnie Prince Charlie's uprising in 1746, the clan system was swept away. The clansmen were still there, but transformed into crofters. Elsewhere, such subsistence smallholders go by the honourable name of 'peasant farmers', with 25 acres (10ha), a kailyard, a cow and some sheep on the hill.

# The Crofters

Under the new system Rents rose, partly to support the landlords' new London lifestyles. Crofting lands were cleared to make way for sheep, and the crofters were forced to relocate, first to the shore and later right out of the country to Canada and Australia. By the late 1800s, they were starting to fight back. In 1882, crofters at the Braes, south of Portree, resisted an eviction. Fifty Glasgow policemen were sent to restore order, and in the 'Battle of the Braes' the crofters retaliated with sticks and stones.

In Glendale, land-starved crofters deliberately let their cattle stray on to neighbouring farms. Government forces and the gunboat *Jackal* were defied by 600 crofters. There were four arrests, including John Macpherson, the 'Glendale Martyr', and a minister, the Reverend D MacCallum. The 'martyrs' received two-month prison sentences. The public outcry that followed saw a newly formed 'Crofters' Party' – a distant forerunner of today's New Labour – send four MPs to Westminster. The first of the Crofting Acts, passed by Gladstone's government, led to less unfair rents and security of tenure.

Today, thanks to those battles of long ago, Glendale and the Braes are inhabited lands where so much of Scotland is bleak and empty. Crofters now have the right to buy, and enjoy subsidies and grants from the government. Few crofts provide enough to live on, without a part-time job on the side. As a result, there's a series of small-scale, off-beat and interesting tourist enterprises along the Glendale Trail.

Peat became the crofters' fuel supply and in a few places it is still being worked today, often where a modern road runs beside one of the remaining peat banks. Above Loch Eishort on this walk you'll see the little triangular stacks, each made from four peats, drying in the wind (and of course getting wet again in the rain). When it burns, it brings the smell of the wild bog-moss right into the house.

LEFT: *Dunvegan village and Loch Dunvegan, Isle of Skye*

## walk directions

1 From the end of the tarmac, the road continues as a track between farm buildings, with a bridge over the **Ramasaig Burn**. After a gate it reaches a shed with a tin roof. Bear right here and follow the left bank of Ramasaig Burn to the shore.

2 Cross the burn at a ford and head up a very steep meadow beside the fence that protects the cliff edge. There's an awkward fence to cross half way up. At the top, above **Ramasaig Cliff**, keep following the fence on the left. It cuts across to the right to protect a notch in the cliff edge. From here (Point ③), you could cut down to the parking areas at the road pass near by.

3 Keep downhill along the cliffside fence. At the bottom, a turf wall off to the right provides another short-cut back to the road. The clifftop walk now bears slightly right around the V-notch of the **Moonen Burn**. A small path crosses the stream and continues uphill to rejoin the clifftop fence, which soon turns slightly inland around another cliff notch. The cliff-edge fence leads up and to the left, to reach **Waterstein Head**. Here there is a trig point, 971ft (296m) above the sea – the second highest sea cliff on Skye. Below you will see Neist Point lighthouse.

4 Return for ¼ mile (400m) down to where the fence bends to the right, then continue ahead through a shallow grassy col for the slight rise to **Beinn Charnach**. Here, bear right to follow a gently rounded grass ridge line parallel with the cliffs. The highest line along the ridge is the driest. A fence runs across, with a grey gate at its highest point, where it passes through a col. Climb over the gate and on up to a cairn on **Beinn na Coinnich**.

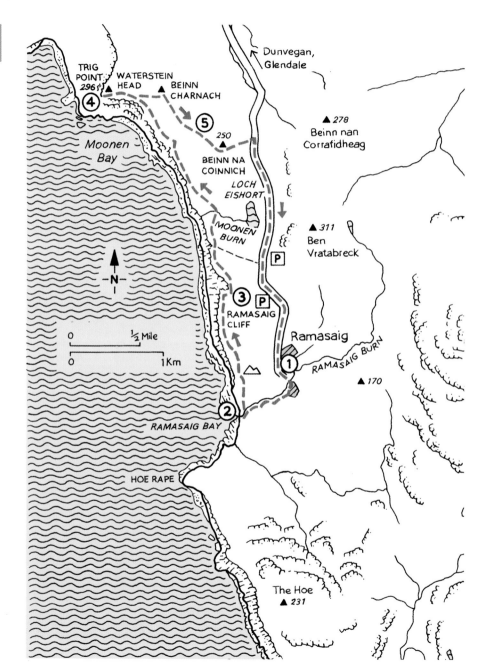

## walk information

| | |
|---|---|
| ➤ **DISTANCE** | 5¾ miles (9.2km) |
| ➤ **MINIMUM TIME** | 3hrs 30min |
| ➤ **ASCENT/GRADIENT** | 1,500ft (457m) ▲▲▲ |
| ➤ **LEVEL OF DIFFICULTY** | 🚶🚶 🚶🚶 🚶 |
| ➤ **PATHS** | Grassy clifftops and moorland, 1 stile |
| ➤ **LANDSCAPE** | Clifftops high above Atlantic Ocean |
| ➤ **SUGGESTED MAP** | OS Explorer 407 Skye – Dunvegan |
| ➤ **START/FINISH** | Grid reference: NG 163443 |
| ➤ **DOG FRIENDLINESS** | Mostly on lead – risk of scaring sheep over cliff edges |
| ➤ **PARKING** | Ramasaig road end or pull-ins at pass ¾ mile (1.2km) farther north |
| ➤ **PUBLIC TOILETS** | None on route |
| ➤ **CONTRIBUTOR** | Ronald Turnbull |

**5** Continue along the slightly rocky plateau for 300yds (274m) to the south east top. Now the Ramasaig road is visible ¼ mile (400m) away on the left. Go down to join a quad bike track heading towards the road. Just before reaching the road, the bike track crosses a swampy col. This shows old and recent peat workings. Turn right, along the road, passing above **Loch Eishort** to the start.

*LEFT: Dunvegan Castle, Isle of Skye*

*Exploring the weird lava landscape*
*of Skye's northern peninsula.*

# Prison and Pinnacle

The rocks of Scotland vary from ancient – about 400 million years – to a great deal older than that, but along the western edge is something quite different. The great eye of the Atlantic Ocean opened at a time that, geologically speaking, is this morning just before breakfast. A mere 60 million years ago, the mid-Atlantic ridge lay just off the Scottish coast. And all along that ridge, new seabed emerged in exotic and interesting volcanic rocks that now form the Arran granite, the basalt of Mull and Skye, and the Skye gabbro.

ABOVE: *Roseroot and alpine vegetation*
RIGHT: *Beinn Edra and the Trotternish Ridge from the Quiraing, Isle of Skye*

## Lava Landscape

Stir together butter and sugar in a saucepan, take the mixture off the heat and it crystallises into fudge. But take the same ingredients and cool them quickly, by tipping them into cold water, for example, and you get the glassy solid we call toffee. Now take a basic silicaceous magma, let it cool over thousands of years deep inside a volcano, and you'll get the rough crystalline gabbro that described on page 58. But let it erupt suddenly at the surface, and it congeals into basalt, which is black, shiny and slippery. It forms a completely different sort of scenery – that of northern Skye.

Basalt lava is a slippery liquid, like milk rather than treacle. This makes it quite different from the lumpy rhyolite lava that formed Glen Coe and the craggy side of Ben Nevis. Basalt lava spreads in wide, shallow layers across the country. After erosion, you get a flat-topped landscape, with long low cliffs at the edges and wide grassy plateaux. Macleod's Tables are lava-layer hills, as is Dun Caan on Raasay.

North of Portree, the lava flowed out over older, softer rocks of Jurassic (dinosaur) age. All along the Trotternish peninsula, the sea has been steadily removing those softer rocks, and the basalt above has been breaking off in hill-sized chunks and slipping downhill and eastwards. The chunks lean over, split apart and erode: the result is some extraordinary scenery, of which the queerest is the Quiraing.

Some of its rock forms, with intriguing names such as the Prison, the Needle and the Fingalian Slab, have been a tourist must-see since Victorian times. As a result, a wide, well-made path leads below these pinnacles, then back along the top.

## walk information

| | |
|---|---|
| ➤ **DISTANCE** | 5¼ miles (8.4km) |
| ➤ **MINIMUM TIME** | 3hrs |
| ➤ **ASCENT/GRADIENT** | 1,200ft (365m) ▲▲▲ |
| ➤ **LEVEL OF DIFFICULTY** | 🚶🚶 🚶🚶 🚶🚶 |
| ➤ **PATHS** | Well-used path, 1 stile |
| ➤ **LANDSCAPE** | Rock towers and pinnacles |
| ➤ **SUGGESTED MAP** | OS Explorer 408 Skye – Trotternish & the Storr |
| ➤ **START/FINISH** | Grid reference: NG 440679 |
| ➤ **DOG FRIENDLINESS** | On leads passing sheep, care on cliff top |
| ➤ **PARKING** | Pull-in, top of pass on Staffin–Uig road. Overflow parking at cemetery ¼ mile (400m) on Staffin side (not available during funerals) |
| ➤ **PUBLIC TOILETS** | Brogaig |
| ➤ **CONTRIBUTOR** | Ronald Turnbull |

## walk directions

1  A well-built path starts at a 'bendy road' sign opposite the lay-by. The jagged tower of grass and rock on the skyline is the Prison. The path crosses the steep landslip slope towards it, with an awkward crossing of a small stream gully on bare rock, then passes a small waterfall high above and heads to the right rather than up into a rocky gap. It turns uphill into the wide col to the left of **the Prison**.

2  The main path does not drop, but goes forward, slightly uphill, crossing an old fence line at a crag foot. It crosses the foot of steep ground, then passes above a small peat pool. Ignore a path forking down right; the main path slants up left into a col where an old wall runs across.

*LEFT: The Quiraing ridge*

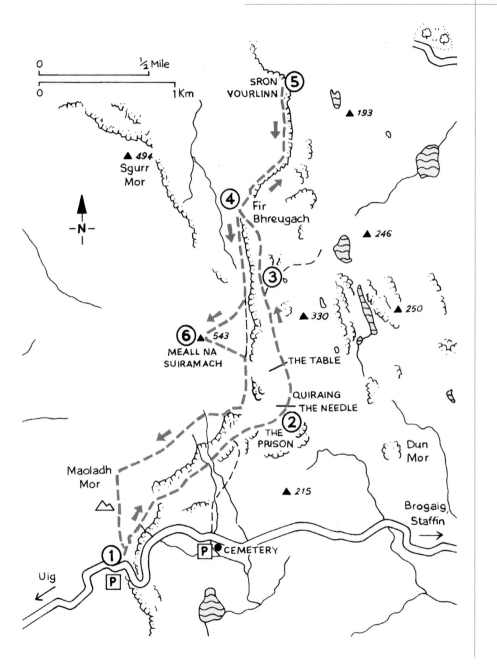

95

3 The path descends into a landslip valley that runs across rather than down the hillside, then slants up left to a col with a stile.

4 Cross and turn right for the excursion to **Sron Vourlinn**. Follow the crest over a slightly rocky section with a short descent beyond, then join the main path along a grassy meadow with a very sudden edge on the right. After the highest point, continue slightly downhill to the north top. Here you can see that the land is still slipping, with a crevasse beside the cliff edge where another narrow section is shortly to peel away. The shelter of the rock crevice grows luxuriant rock rose, rowan and valerian.

5 Return to the col with the stile (Point ④) and continue uphill. The drops are now on your left, as you look down towards the pinnacles surrounding the Table. After passing broken ground on the right, you come to a fallen wall, part of which appears from below as a cairn. The path continues next to the cliff edge on the left; you can fork off right, directly uphill, to the summit trig point on **Meall na Suiramach**.

6 Follow a broad, gentle path slightly downhill to a cairn at the cliff edge. You now look straight down on to **the Table**, 100ft (30m) below. Turn right on the wide path. After a mile (1.6km), the path starts to descend alongside the cliff edge. As the edge turns half right, you should turn fully right. The path is faint, but reappears ahead contouring around the fairly steep grass slope. Once above the car park it turns straight downhill for a final steep descent.

*BELOW: Overlooking the Quiraing*

*The castle on the island in the loch is the heart of Rothiemurchus Forest.*

# Loch an Eilein's Castle and Ord Ban

ABOVE: *Castle ruins by Loch an Eilein*

A secluded island castle, surrounded by ancient pines, and the mountains rising behind – you hardly have to bother with the rest of Scotland as Loch an Eilean has it all. This walk will reveal every aspect of this beautiful loch, plus the bonus of seeing Loch Gamhna.

## Castle for Cattle Thieves

Loch an Eilein Castle was built by John Comyn II, known as the Red Comyn, in the 13th century. It guards the strategic cattle-stealing route, the Rathad nam Meirleach, which runs along the shore of the loch. Locals used to keep a cow tied to a tree in hope that the raiders would take that and leave the rest alone. The three murderers of a Macintosh chieftain were imprisoned in chains here for seven years, before being executed in 1531. The castle was most recently fought over in 1690. Grizzel Mhor (Big Grizelda), the chieftain's wife, held it for Clan Grant against the King in 1690. There is said to be an underwater zig-zag causeway leading out to the island.

## Life in the Pines

Walk quietly with binoculars and you may see some of the unique birdlife of the forest. The crested tit resembles the more familiar coal tit, with brown body and striped head, but with the Mohican hair-style effect of its crest. It nests in holes in old, rotten trees, so will only be found in wild forest. The Scottish crossbill, found only in Scotland, has a parrot-like beak, adapted for cracking open pine cones. The capercaillie is the large grouse of the forest and its name means 'horse of the woods'. The male challenges and intimidates other males with a noise like the clip-clop of hooves, or like a wine-bottle being opened. Your only real chance of seeing it in the wild is at dawn, in spring, at the RSPB reserve at Loch Garten (better known for its ospreys).

## Osprey Island

Ospreys used to nest in the castle ruins. An egg collector once swam across wearing nothing but his cap, which he used to bring back his plunder. Ospreys are back in the Cairngorms, and though they won't return to this over-public island, you might see them elsewhere plunging feet-first as they strike for a trout.

*LEFT AND RIGHT: Countryside and marshland around Loch an Eilein*

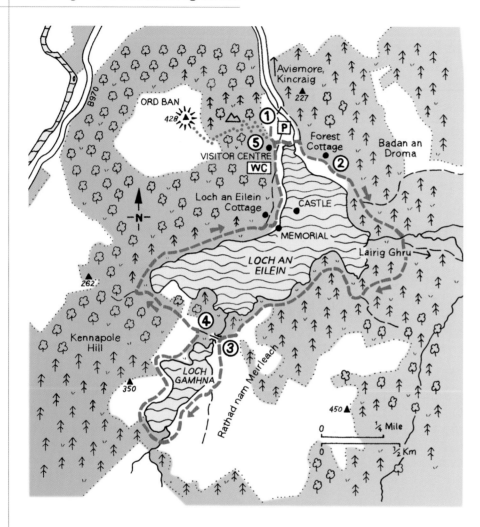

## walk information

| | |
|---|---|
| ➤ **DISTANCE** | 4¼ miles (6.8km) |
| ➤ **MINIMUM TIME** | 1hr 45min |
| ➤ **ASCENT/GRADIENT** | 100ft (30m) |
| ➤ **LEVEL OF DIFFICULTY** | 🚶 🚶 🚶 |
| ➤ **PATHS** | Wide, smooth paths, optional steep hill with high ladder stile |
| ➤ **LANDSCAPE** | Ancient pine forest around loch |
| ➤ **SUGGESTED MAP** | OS Explorer 403 Cairn Gorm & Aviemore |
| ➤ **START/FINISH** | Grid reference: NH 897084 |
| ➤ **DOG FRIENDLINESS** | On leads on Rothiemurchus Estate |
| ➤ **PARKING** | Estate car park near Loch an Eilein |
| ➤ **PUBLIC TOILETS** | Visitor centre |
| ➤ **CONTRIBUTOR** | Ronald Turnbull |

*RIGHT: Sunset over Loch an Eilein*

## walk directions

**1** From the end of the car park at the beginning of the walk, a made-up path leads to the visitor centre. Turn left to cross the end of **Loch an Eilein**, then turn right on a smooth, sandy track. The loch shore is near by on the right. There are small paths leading down to it if you wish to visit. Just past a red-roofed house, a deer fence runs across, with a gate.

**2** The track now becomes a wide, smooth path, which runs close to the loch side. After a bridge, the main track forks right to pass a bench backed by a flat boulder. The smaller path on the left leads high into the hills and through the famous pass of the **Lairig Ghru**, eventually to Braemar. After crossing a stream at a low concrete footbridge, the path bends right for 120yds (110m) to a junction. Just beyond is a footbridge with wooden handrails.

3 To shorten the walk, cross this footbridge and continue along the main track, passing Point ④ in another 170yds (155m). For a longer walk, turn left before the footbridge on to a narrower path that will pass around **Loch Gamhna**. This second loch soon appears on your right-hand side. Where the path forks, keep right to pass along the loch side, across its head (rather boggy) and back along its further side, to rejoin the wider path around **Loch an Eilein**. Turn left here.

4 Continue around Loch an Eilein, with the water on your right, to a reedy corner of the loch and a bench. About 55yds (51m) further, the path turns sharply right, signposted 'footpath'. After a gate, turn right to the loch side and a **memorial** to Major General Brook Rice, who drowned here while skating. Follow the shore to the point opposite the castle, then back up to the wide track above. A deer fence on the left leads back to the visitor centre.

5 From here, a stiff climb (around 500ft/152m) can be made on to the rocky little hill of **Ord Ban**, a superb viewpoint. Cross a ladder stile immediately to the right of the toilet block and follow the deer fence to the right for 150yds (137m), to a point behind the car park. Just behind one of the lowest birches on the slope, a small path zig-zags up the steep slope. It slants to the left to avoid crags, then crosses a small rock slab (take care if wet) and continues on to the summit. Descend by the same path.

*Above the Great Glen on the road the English built and over which Bonnie Prince Charlie marched.*

# Up and Down the Corrieyairack

The most striking feature of Scotland's geography is the 2,000-ft (610-m) deep Great Glen. It runs perfectly straight from Fort William to Inverness as if a giant ploughshare had been dragged across the country. This walk allows you to explore a small but significant section of it.

ABOVE: *Detail of biblical carvings on the doorway of the Benedictine Abbey of 1876 in Fort Augustus*
RIGHT: *The mountains of Stob A'Ghrianain and Beinn Bhan rise from the Great Glen*

## Scotland's San Andreas

Around 400 million years ago, the northern part of Scotland slipped 65 miles (105km) to the left. Looking across from Corrieyairack, you'd have seen ground that's now the Island of Mull. The Great Glen represents a tear-fault, similar to the San Andreas Fault in California, but no longer active, so that there isn't going to be any Fort Augustus Earthquake. Where two ground masses slide past each other, the rock where they touch is shattered. Rivers and glaciers have worn away this broken rock to make the striking valley.

## Wade's Ways

After the uprising of 1715, General Wade became the military commander of Scotland. He constructed and repaired forts along the Great Glen at Fort William, Fort Augustus and Inverness, as well as at Ruthven on the present A9 and Glenelg. To link them, he built 260 miles (around 418km) of roads across the Highlands. The most spectacular of these was the one through the Corrieyairack Pass, rising to 2,500ft (762m) to link the Great Glen with the Spey.

The construction was little changed since Roman times. Large rocks were jammed together into a firm bed, up to 15ft (4.5m) wide, and then surfaced with smaller stones and gravel packed down. Modern path-builders know that however well you build it, if it's got water running down it turns into a stream. Wade paid particular attention to drainage. The 500 soldiers working through the summer of 1731 got a bonus of 6d a day – about £5 in today's money – and celebrated its completion with a barbecue of six oxen.

The chieftains worried that the roads would soften their people, making them unfit for raids across rough country. However, they soon came to appreciate the convenience. 'If you'd seen these roads before they were made, You'd lift up your hands and bless General Wade.'

And when Prince Charles Stuart landed 14 years later, it was the Jacobite army that marched triumphantly across the Corrieyairack. At the Speyside end of the pass, a small and ill-prepared force under General John Cope fled before him into England. As a result, a new Wade rhyme was inserted, temporarily, into the National Anthem itself: 'God grant that Marshal Wade, May by Thy mighty aid, Victory bring, May he sedition hush, and like a torrent rush, Rebellious Scots to crush, God save the King.'

## walk directions

1 A track leads round to the left of the burial ground to meet a minor road. Turn right for about ¼ mile (400m), to the foot of a rather rubbly track signposted for the Corrieyairack Pass. After some 50yds (46m), the track passes through a gate, getting much easier and, soon, the right of way joins a smoother track coming up from **Culachy House**.

2 After another ¼ mile (400m), a gate leads out on to the open hill. About 350yds (320m) further on, the track passes under high-tension wires. At once, bear left across a grassy meadow. As this drops towards a stream, you will see a green track slanting down to the right. Bear left off the track to pass the corner of a deer fence, where a small path continues down to the stream. Cross and turn downstream on an old grassy track. It recrosses the stream and passes under the high power line to a bend with a sudden view across deep and wooded **Glen Tarff**.

3 Turn right to cross over a high stone bridge. A disused track climbs through birch woods then, as a terraced shelf, across the high side of Glen Tarff. A side stream forms a wooded re-entrant ahead. The old track contours in to this and crosses below a narrow waterfall – the former bridge has disappeared.

4 Contour out across the steep slope to pick up the old track as it restarts. It runs gently uphill to a gateless gateway in a fence. Turn up the fence to another gateway, 150yds (137m) above. Here, turn left for 20yds (18m) to the brink of another stream hollow. (Its delightful Gaelic name – Sidhean Ceum na Goibhre – means 'Fairy Goat-step'.)

LEFT: *Looking down the Great Glen towards the Caledonian Canal and Loch Oich*

Don't go into this, but turn uphill alongside it, through pathless bracken, to its top. A deer fence is just above; turn left alongside it to go through a nearby gate, then left beside the fence. When it turns downhill, a green path continues ahead, gently uphill through heather. Far ahead and above, pylons crossing the skyline mark the **Corrieyairack Pass**. The path bends right to join the Corrieyairack track just above.

**5** Turn right. The track passes a knoll on the right, where a small cairn marks the highest point of this walk. It then descends in sweeping curves for 1¼ miles (2km). The pass is still technically a road, and where it crosses a stream, a Highways Authority sign warns motorists coming up it of the various difficulties and dangers ahead. From here, the track climbs gently to rejoin the upward route. At the final bend, a stile offers a short cut through (rather than round) the ancient burial ground.

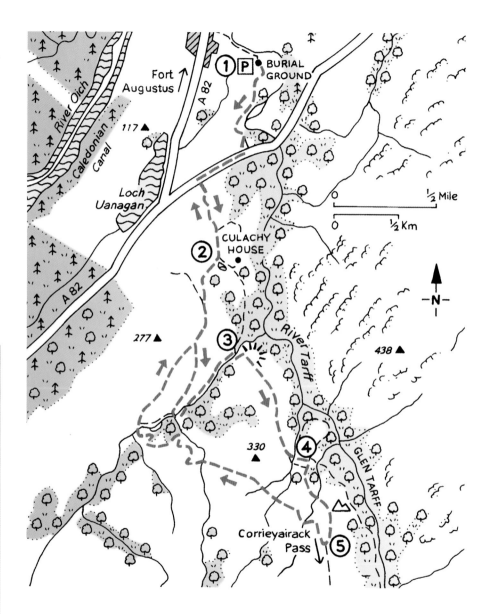

## walk information

| | |
|---|---|
| ➤ **DISTANCE** | 7¼ miles (11.7km) |
| ➤ **MINIMUM TIME** | 4hrs |
| ➤ **ASCENT/GRADIENT** | 1,300ft (395m) ▲ ▲ ▲ |
| ➤ **LEVEL OF DIFFICULTY** | 材 材 材 |
| ➤ **PATHS** | Tracks, one vanished pathless section, 2 stiles |
| ➤ **LANDSCAPE** | Foothills of Monadhliath, birchwood hollows |
| ➤ **SUGGESTED MAP** | OS Explorer 400 Loch Lochy & Glen Roy |
| ➤ **START/FINISH** | Grid reference: NH 378080 |
| ➤ **DOG FRIENDLINESS** | Off lead, unless passing sheep |
| ➤ **PARKING** | Southern edge of Fort Augustus, signed lane leads off A82 to burial ground |
| ➤ **PUBLIC TOILETS** | Fort Augustus |
| ➤ **CONTRIBUTOR** | Ronald Turnbull |

*A walk around the many inlets*
*of the Shieldaig peninsula.*

# The Shores of Loch Shieldaig

ABOVE: *Playing the bagpipes on*
*Pitlochry Dam*

The Shieldaig peninsula separates inner and outer Loch Torridon, and at every turn there's a new view – up the loch to Liathach and the less-known hills to the south, out across the sea to Skye and Raasay, or into a sheltered bay with a cluster of eider or the sleek head of a seal.

## Scotland's Scourge

In Gaelic she's meanbh-chuileag, the tiny fly, but she's better known as the mighty midge, Scotland's scourge. I say 'she' as the male is an altogether weaker creature, content with a suck of bog myrtle, a brief dance in the summer haze and death among the heather stalks. It's the female that needs a blood meal in order to lay her eggs. The blood host could be a deer, a sheep, a grouse, or, of course, you. The larvae hatch in wet peat moss, which is all too common in western Scotland. They are able to absorb oxygen even from such waterlogged surroundings.

## Midgie Prince

Bonnie Prince Charlie, wandering Scotland in the damp summer of 1746, was mildly inconvenienced by the pursuing redcoats; his real enemy was the midge. On Benbecula, crouching under a rock in the rain, on a muggy June day, he lost his customary poise and gave way to 'hideous cries and complaints'. His remedy was brandy when brandy was to be had, and otherwise whisky. During his flight through the heather he got through as much as a bottle a day. Indeed, his alcoholism in later life can in part be blamed on the midge.

There's a historical mystery over the midge. Dr Johnson, touring just 27 years later, didn't notice the midge at all. The poet Samuel Taylor Coleridge, walking the Great Glen in 1803, found them mildly annoying, but the bed-bugs were much worse. By 1872, the midges were bad enough to completely ruin one of Queen Victoria's picnics. This increase in the midge may be down to the Highland Clearances. Glens formerly farmed became their bog breeding grounds. But the worst midge story of all is said to have happened at Gairloch. A replacement minister, the Revd John Morrison, was sent to the Presbyterian church there in 1711, and the congregation so disapproved of his sermon that they stripped him naked, tied him to a tree and left him overnight for the midges!

*LEFT: Loch Shieldaig*

## walk directions

1 Follow the village street north, along the shoreline. At the village end it rises slightly, with another parking area, and a **war memorial** above on the right.

2 In front of the village school, turn right up a rough track. The track passes a couple of houses to turn left. In another 100yds (91m) it divides; here the main track for **Rubha Lodge** forks off left, but your route bears right, passing to the right of a glacier-smoothed rock knoll. The terraced path runs through birch woods at first, with **Loch Shieldaig** below on the left. It passes above two rocky bays, then strikes across a peat bog, bright in mid-summer with bell heather and the fluffy white tops of cotton grass. In the middle of this flat area, the path divides at a cairn.

## walk information

| | |
|---|---|
| ➤ **DISTANCE** | 3¼ miles (5.3km) |
| ➤ **MINIMUM TIME** | 1hr 45min |
| ➤ **ASCENT/GRADIENT** | 500ft (152m) ▲ ▲ ▲ |
| ➤ **LEVEL OF DIFFICULTY** | 🚶 🚶 🚶 |
| ➤ **PATHS** | Well-made, old paths, 1 rough section |
| ➤ **LANDSCAPE** | Saltwater views up Loch Torridon and down Loch Shieldaig |
| ➤ **SUGGESTED MAP** | OS Explorer 428 Kyle of Lochalsh |
| ➤ **START/FINISH** | Grid reference: NG 814538 |
| ➤ **DOG FRIENDLINESS** | On leads in village and when passing livestock |
| ➤ **PARKING** | South end of Shieldaig village, opposite shop and hotel |
| ➤ **PUBLIC TOILETS** | North end of village (another car park) |
| ➤ **CONTRIBUTOR** | Ronald Turnbull |

RIGHT: *Shieldaig village on the shoreline*

3 The right-hand path runs along the left edge of the peaty area, with rocky ground above on its left, then next to birch trees for 50yds (46m). Look out for the point where its pink gravel surface becomes peaty, with a rock formation like a low ruin on the right, because here is an easily-missed path junction.

4 What seems like the main footpath, ahead and slightly downhill, peters out eventually. The correct path forks off to the left, slanting up on to the higher ground just above. The path is now clear, crossing slabby ground in the direction of the peninsula's trig point, ¼ mile (400m) away. After 220yds (201m), it rises slightly to a gateway in a former fence. Aiming right of the trig point, it crosses a small heather moor. At a broken wall, the path turns down, right, through a gap to the top of a grassy meadow. The first of the two shoreline cottages, **Bad-callda**, is just below. Rough paths lead to the left across the boggy top of the meadow and above a birchwood, with the trig point just above on the left. Keep going forward at the same level to a heather knoll, with a pole on it. Just below you is a second cottage, **Camas-ruadh**.

5 The footpath zig-zags down between rocks. White paint spots lead round to the right of the cottage and its shed, to join a clear path coming from the cottage. The return path is easy to follow, with the cottage's phone line always near by on the left. After ½ mile (800m), it rejoins the outward route at the cairn, Point ③.

# Walking in Safety

All these walks are suitable for any reasonably fit person, but less experienced walkers should try the easier walks first. Route finding is usually straightforward, but you will find that an Ordnance Survey map is a useful addition to the route maps and descriptions.

# Risks

Although each walk here has been researched with a view to minimising the risks to the walkers who follow its route, no walk in the countryside can be considered to be completely free from risk. Walking in the outdoors will always require a degree of common sense and judgement to ensure that it is as safe as possible.

- Be particularly careful on cliff paths and in upland terrain, where the consequences of a slip can be very serious.
- Remember to always check tidal conditions before setting off for a walk along the seashore.
- Some sections of route are by, or cross, busy roads. Take care and remember traffic is a danger, even on minor country lanes.
- Be careful around farmyard machinery and livestock, especially if you have children with you.
- Be aware of the consequences of changes in the weather and check the forecast before you set out. Carry spare clothing and a torch if you are walking in the winter months. Remember the weather can change very quickly at any time of the year, and in moorland and heathland areas, mist and fog can make route finding much harder. Don't set out in these conditions unless you are confident of your navigation skills in poor visibility. In summer, remember to take account of the heat and sun; wear a hat and sunscreen, and carry spare water.
- On walks away from centres of population, you should carry a whistle and survival bag. If you do have an accident requiring the emergency services, make a note of your position as accurately as possible and dial 999.

## Acknowledgements

All photographs are held in the Association's own picture library (AA World Photo Library) and were taken by the following photographers:

Sue Anderson 2/3, 31, 51, 67; Adrian Baker 71; Jeff Beazley 82, 108/9, 111; Jim Carnie 12, 28/9, 52; Steve Day 7cl, 13, 14r, 14l, 17, 21, 32, 50, 54, 56l, 107; Robert Eames 96; Eric Ellington 63, 86, 87, 97, 98, 99; Richard G. Elliot 7cr, 53, 72, 76, 78, 84; Derek Forss 16, 72/3, 74; Jim Henderson 7r, 40, 42, 47, 58, 64, 66; A. J. Hopkins 22, 24/5, 92, 93, 101; Ken Paterson 38/9, 43, 44/5, 68,102/3; Rod Richards 102; Peter Sharpe 49; Jonathan Smith 34, 36; Ronald Weir 11, 23, 41, 56r, 68/9, 91; Stephen Whitehorne 5, 6, 10, 18/9, 27, 33, 44, 57, 59, 61, 62/3, 71, 81, 88/9, 94, 104/5; Harry Williams 37.

Every effort has been made to trace the copyright holders, and we apologise in advance for any unintentional omissions or errors. We would be pleased to apply any corrections in any following edition of this publication.